C000100009

Django for Professionals

Production websites with Python & Django

William S. Vincent

Django for Professionals

Production websites with Python & Django

William S. Vincent

learndjango.com

ISBN-13: 978-1735467238

Also By William S. Vincent

Django for Beginners

Django for APIs

Contents

Introduction

Welcome to *Django for Professionals*, a guide to building professional websites with the Django web framework[1]. There is a massive gulf between building simple "toy apps" that can be created and deployed quickly and what it takes to build a "production-ready" web application suitable for deployment to thousands or even millions of users. This book will show you to how to bridge that gap.

When you first install Django and create a new project the default settings are geared towards fast local development. And this makes sense: there's no need to add all the additional features required of a large website until you know you need them. These defaults include SQLite as the default database, a local web server, local static asset hosting, built-in User model, and DEBUG mode turned on.

But for a production project many, if not most, of these settings must be reconfigured. And even then there can be a frustrating lack of agreement among the experts. For example, what's the best production database to use? Many Django developers, myself included, choose PostgreSQL. It is what we will use in this book. However an argument can be made for MySQL depending on the project. It really does all depend on the specific requirements of a project.

Rather than overwhelm the reader with the full array of choices available this book shows one approach, grounded in current Django community best practices, for building a professional website. The topics covered include using Docker for local development and deployment, PostgreSQL, a custom user model, robust user authentication flow with email, comprehensive testing, environment variables, security and performance improvements, and more.

By the end of this book you will have built a professional website and learned all the necessary steps to do so. Whether you are starting a new project that hopes to be as large as Instagram (currently the largest Django website in the world) or making much-needed updates to an existing Django project, you will have the tools and knowledge to do so.

---

[1]https://djangoproject.com

Prerequisites

If you're brand-new to either Django or web development, this is not the book for you. The pace will be far too fast. While you *could* read along, copy all the code, and have a working website at the end, I instead recommend starting with my book Django for Beginners[2]. It starts with the very basics and progressively introduces concepts via building five increasingly complex Django applications. After completing that book you will be ready for success with this book.

I have also written a book on transforming Django websites into web APIs called Django for APIs[3]. In practice most Django developers work in teams with other developers and focus on back-end APIs, not full-stack web applications that require dedicated JavaScript front-ends. Reading *Django for APIs* is therefore helpful to your education as a Django developer, but not required before reading this book.

We will use Docker throughout most of this book but still rely, briefly, on having Python 3, Django, and Pipenv installed locally. Git is also a necessary part of the developer toolchain. Finally, we will be using the command line extensively in this book as well so if you need a refresher on it, please see here[4].

Book Structure

Chapter 1 starts with an introduction to Docker and explores how to "Dockerize" a traditional Django project. In *Chapter* 2 PostgreSQL is introduced, a production-ready database that we can run locally within our Docker environment. Then *Chapter* 3 starts the main project in the book: an online Bookstore featuring a custom user model, search, image uploads, permissions, and a host of other goodies.

Chapter 4 focuses on building out a Pages app for a basic homepage along with robust testing which is included with every new feature on the site. In *Chapter* 5 a complete user registration flow is implemented from scratch using the built-in auth app for sign up, log in, and log out.

---

[2]https://djangoforbeginners.com
[3]https://djangoforapis.com
[4]https://learndjango.com/tutorials/terminal-command-line-beginners

Chapter 6 introduces proper static asset configuration for CSS, JavaScript, and images as well as the addition of Bootstrap for styling.

In *Chapter* 7 the focus shifts to advanced user registration, namely including email-only log in and social authentication via the third-party `django-allauth` package. *Chapter* 8 introduces environment variables, a key component of Twelve-Factor App development and a best practice widely used in the web development community. Rounding out the set up of our project, *Chapter* 9 focuses on email and adding a dedicated third-party provider.

The structure of the first half of the book is intentional. When it comes time to build your own Django projects, chances are you will be repeating many of the same steps from Chapters 3-9. After all, every new project needs proper configuration, user authentication, and environment variables. So treat these chapters as your detailed explanation and guide. The second half of the book focuses on specific features related to our Bookstore website.

Chapter 10 starts with building out the models, tests, and pages for our Bookstore via a `Books` app. There is also a discussion of URLs and switching from `id` to a slug to a UUID (Universally Unique IDentifier) in the URLs. *Chapter* 11 features the addition of reviews to our Bookstore and a discussion of foreign keys.

In *Chapter* 12 image-uploading is added and in *Chapter* 13 permissions are set across the site to lock it down. For any site but especially e-commerce, search is a vital component and *Chapter* 14 walks through building a form and increasingly complex search filters for the site.

In *Chapter* 15 the focus switches to performance optimizations including the addition of `django-debug-toolbar` to inspect queries and templates, database indexes, front-end assets, and multiple built-in caching options. *Chapter* 16 covers security in Django, both the built-in options as well as additional configurations that can-and should-be added for a production environment. The final section, *Chapter* 17, is on deployment, the standard upgrades needed to migrate away from the Django web server, local static file handling, and configuring `ALLOWED_HOSTS`.

The *Conclusion* touches upon various next steps to take with the project and additional Django best practices.

Book Layout

There are many code examples in this book, which are formatted as follows:

Code

```python
# This is Python code
print(Hello, World)
```

For brevity we will use dots ... to denote existing code that remains unchanged, for example, in a function we are updating.

Code

```python
def make_my_website:
    ...
    print("All done!")
```

We will also use the command line console frequently to execute commands, which take the form of a $ prefix in traditional Unix style.

Command Line

```
$ echo "hello, world"
```

The result of this particular command in the next line will state:

Command Line

```
"hello, world"
```

Typically both a command and its output will be combined for brevity. The command will always be prefaced by a $ and the output will not. For example, the command and result above would be represented as follows:

Command Line

```
$ echo "hello, world"
hello, world
```

Text Editor

A modern text editor is a must-have part of any software developer's toolkit. Among other features they come with plug-ins that help format and correct errors in Python code. Popular options include Black[5], autopep8[6], and YAPF[7].

Seasoned developers may still prefer using Vim[8] or Emacs[9], but newcomers and increasingly experienced programmers as well prefer modern text editors such as VSCode[10], Atom[11], Sublime Text[12], or PyCharm[13].

Conclusion

Django is an excellent choice for any developer who wants to build modern, robust web applications with a minimal amount of code. It is popular, under active development, and thoroughly battle-tested by the largest websites in the world.

Complete source code for the book can be found in the official Github repository[14].

In the next chapter we'll learn how to configure any computer for Django development with Docker.

---

[5] https://github.com/ambv/black

[6] https://github.com/hhatto/autopep8

[7] https://github.com/google/yapf

[8] https://www.vim.org/

[9] https://www.gnu.org/software/emacs/

[10] https://code.visualstudio.com/

[11] https://atom.io/

[12] https://www.sublimetext.com/

[13] https://www.jetbrains.com/pycharm/

[14] https://github.com/wsvincent/djangoforprofessionals

Chapter 1: Docker

Properly configuring a local development environment remains a steep challenge despite all the other advances in modern programming. There are simply too many variables: different computers, operating systems, versions of Django, virtual environment options, and so on. When you add in the challenge of working in a team environment where everyone needs to have the same set up the problem only magnifies.

In recent years a solution has emerged: Docker[15]. Although only a few years old, Docker has quickly become the default choice for many developers working on production-level projects.

With Docker it's finally possible to faithfully and dependably reproduce a production environment locally, everything from the proper Python version to installing Django and running additional services like a production-level database. This means it no longer matter if you are on a Mac, Windows, or Linux computer. Everything is running within Docker itself.

Docker also makes collaboration in teams exponentially easier. Gone are the days of sharing long, out-of-date `README` files for adding a new developer to a group project. Instead with Docker you simply share two files–a `Dockerfile` and `docker-compose.yml` file–and the developer can have confidence that their local development environment is exactly the same as the rest of the team.

Docker is not a perfect technology. It is still relatively new, complex under-the-hood, and under active development. But the promise that it aspires to–a consistent and shareable developer environment, that can be run either locally on any computer or deployed to any server–makes it a solid choice.

In this chapter we'll learn a little bit more about Docker itself and "Dockerize" our first Django project.

---

[15]https://www.docker.com/

What is Docker?

Docker is a way to isolate an entire operating system via Linux containers which are a type of virtualization[16]. Virtualization has its roots at the beginning of computer science when large, expensive mainframe computers were the norm. How could multiple programmers use the same single machine? The answer was virtualization and specifically virtual machines[17] which are complete copies of a computer system from the operating system on up.

If you rent space on a cloud provider like Amazon Web Services (AWS)[18] they are typically not providing you with a dedicated piece of hardware. Instead you are sharing one physical server with other clients. But because each client has their virtual machine running on the server, it appears to the client as if they have their own server.

This technology is what makes it possible to quickly add or remove servers from a cloud provider. It's largely software behind the scenes, not actual hardware being changed.

What's the downside to a virtual machine? Size and speed. A typical guest operating system can easily take up 700MB of size. So if one physical server supports three virtual machines, that's at least 2.1GB of disk space taken up along with separate needs for CPU and memory resources.

Enter Docker. The key idea is that most computers rely on the same Linux[19] operating system, so what if we virtualized from the Linux layer up[20] instead? Wouldn't that provide a lightweight, faster way to duplicate much of the same functionality? The answer is yes. And in recent years Linux containers[21] have become widely popular. For most applications–especially web applications–a virtual machine provides far more resources than are needed and a container is more than sufficient.

This, fundamentally, is what Docker is: a way to implement Linux containers!

An analogy we can use here is that of homes and apartments. Virtual Machines are like homes: stand-alone buildings with their own infrastructure including plumbing and heating, as well as

---

[16]https://en.wikipedia.org/wiki/Virtualization
[17]https://en.wikipedia.org/wiki/Virtual_machine
[18]https://aws.amazon.com/
[19]https://en.wikipedia.org/wiki/Linux
[20]https://en.wikipedia.org/wiki/Operating-system-level_virtualization
[21]https://en.wikipedia.org/wiki/Linux_containers

a kitchen, bathrooms, bedrooms, and so on. Docker containers are like apartments: they share common infrastructure like plumbing and heating, but come in various sizes that match the exact needs of an owner.

Containers vs. Virtual Environments

As a Python programmer you should already familiar with the concept of virtual environments, which are a way to isolate Python packages. Thanks to virtual environments, one computer can run multiple projects locally. For example, Project A might use Python 3.4 and Django 1.11 among other dependencies; whereas Project B uses Python 3.8 and Django 3.1. By configuring a dedicated virtual environment for each project we can manage these different software packages while not polluting our global environment.

Confusingly there are multiple popular tools right now to implement virtual environments: everything from `virtualenv` to `venv` to `Pipenv`, but fundamentally they all do the same thing.

The important distinction between virtual environments and Docker is that virtual environments *can only isolate Python packages*. They cannot isolate non-Python software like a PostgreSQL or MySQL database. And they still rely on a global, system-level installation of Python (in other words, on your computer). The virtual environment points to an existing Python installation; it does not contain Python itself.

Linux containers go a step further and isolate the entire operating system, not just the Python parts. In other words, we will install Python itself within Docker as well as install and run a production-level database.

Docker itself is a complex topic and we won't dive that deep into it in this book, however understanding its background and key components is important. If you'd like to learn more about it, I recommend the Dive into Docker video course[22].

---

[22]https://diveintodocker.com/ref-dfp

Install Docker

Ok, enough theory. Let's start using Docker and Django together. The first step is to sign up for a free account on Docker Hub[23] and then install the Docker desktop app on your local machine:

- Docker for Mac[24]
- Docker for Windows[25]
- Docker for Linux[26]

This download might take some time to download as it is a big file! Feel free to stretch your legs at this point.

Note that the Linux version has the user as `root`, in other words, you can do anything. This is often not ideal and you can set Docker to run as a non-root user[27] if so desired.

Once Docker is done installing we can confirm the correct version is running by typing the command `docker --version` on the command line. It should be at least version 18.

Command Line

```
$ docker --version
Docker version 19.03.12, build 48a66213fe
```

Docker is often used with an additional tool, Docker Compose[28], to help automate commands. Docker Compose is included with Mac and Windows downloads but if you are on Linux you will need to add it manually. You can do this by running the command `sudo pip install docker-compose` after your Docker installation is complete.

---

[23] https://hub.docker.com/signup
[24] https://hub.docker.com/editions/community/docker-ce-desktop-mac
[25] https://hub.docker.com/editions/community/docker-ce-desktop-windows
[26] https://docs.docker.com/install/
[27] https://docs.docker.com/engine/install/linux-postinstall/
[28] https://docs.docker.com/compose/

Docker Hello, World

Docker ships with its own "Hello, World" image that is a helpful first step to run. On the command line type docker run hello-world. This will download an official Docker image and then run it within a container. We'll discuss both images and containers in a moment.

Command Line

```
$ docker run hello-world
Unable to find image 'hello-world:latest' locally
latest: Pulling from library/hello-world
1b930d010525: Pull complete
Digest: sha256:b8ba256769a0ac28dd126d584e0a2011cd2877f3f76e093a7ae560f2a5301c00
Status: Downloaded newer image for hello-world:latest

Hello from Docker!
This message shows that your installation appears to be working correctly.

To generate this message, Docker took the following steps:
 1. The Docker client contacted the Docker daemon.
 2. The Docker daemon pulled the "hello-world" image from the Docker Hub.
    (amd64)
 3. The Docker daemon created a new container from that image which runs the
    executable that produces the output you are currently reading.
 4. The Docker daemon streamed that output to the Docker client, which sent it
    to your terminal.

To try something more ambitious, you can run an Ubuntu container with:
 $ docker run -it ubuntu bash

Share images, automate workflows, and more with a free Docker ID:
 https://hub.docker.com/

For more examples and ideas, visit:
 https://docs.docker.com/get-started/
```

The command docker info lets us inspect Docker. It will contain a lot of output but focus on the top lines which show we now have 1 container which is stopped and 1 image.

Command Line

```
$ docker info
Client:
 Debug Mode: false

Server:
 Containers: 1
  Running: 0
  Paused: 0
  Stopped: 1
 Images: 1
...
```

This means Docker is successfully installed and running.

Django Hello, World

Now we will create a Django "Hello, World" project that runs locally on our computer and then move it entirely within Docker so you can see how all the pieces fit together.

The first step is to choose a location for our code. This can be anywhere on your computer, but if you are on a Mac, an easy-to-find location is the Desktop. From the command line navigate to the Desktop and create a code directory for all the code examples in this book.

Command Line

```
$ cd ~/Desktop
$ mkdir code && cd code
```

Then create a hello directory for this example and install Django using Pipenv which creates both a Pipfile and a Pipfile.lock file. Activate the virtual environment with the shell command.

Command Line

```
$ mkdir hello && cd hello
$ pipenv install django~=3.1.0
$ pipenv shell
(hello) $
```

> If you need help installing Pipenv or Python 3 you can find more details here[a].
>
>   [a]https://djangoforbeginners.com/initial-setup/

Now we can use the `startproject` command to create a new Django project called `config`. Adding a period, `.`, at the end of the command is an optional step but one many Django developers do. Without the period Django adds an additional directory to the project; with the period it does not.

Finally use the `migrate` command to initialize the database and start the local web server with the `runserver` command.

Command Line

```
(hello) $ django-admin startproject config .
(hello) $ python manage.py migrate
(hello) $ python manage.py runserver
```

Assuming everything worked correctly you should now be able to navigate to see the Django Welcome page at `http://127.0.0.1:8000/` in your web browser.

Django welcome page

Pages App

Now we will make a simple homepage by creating a dedicated pages app for it. Stop the local server by typing Control+c and then use the startapp command appending our desired pages name.

```
(hello) $ python manage.py startapp pages
```

Django automatically installs a new `pages` directory and several files for us. But even though the app has been created our `config` won't recognize it until we add it to the `INSTALLED_APPS` config within the `config/settings.py` file. Django loads apps from top to bottom so generally speaking it's a good practice to add new apps below built-in apps they might rely on such as `admin`, `auth`, and all the rest.

Code

```
# config/settings.py
INSTALLED_APPS = [
    'django.contrib.admin',
    'django.contrib.auth',
    'django.contrib.contenttypes',
    'django.contrib.sessions',
    'django.contrib.messages',
    'django.contrib.staticfiles',
    'pages', # new
]
```

Now we can set the URL route for the `pages` app. Since we want our message to appear on the homepage we'll use the empty string `''`. Don't forget to add the `include` import on the second line as well.

Code

```
# config/urls.py
from django.contrib import admin
from django.urls import path, include # new

urlpatterns = [
    path('admin/', admin.site.urls),
    path('', include('pages.urls')), # new
]
```

Rather than set up a template at this point we can just hardcode a message in our view layer at
pages/views.py which will output the string "Hello, World!".

Code

```
# pages/views.py
from django.http import HttpResponse


def home_page_view(request):
    return HttpResponse('Hello, World!')
```

What's next? Our last step is to create a urls.py file within the pages app and link it to home_-
page_view. If you are on an Mac or Linux computer the touch command can be used from the
command line to create new files. On Windows create the new file with your text editor.

Command Line

```
(hello) $ touch pages/urls.py
```

Within your text editor import path on the top line, add the home_page_view, and then set its
route to again be the empty string of ''. Note that we also provide an optional name, home, for
this route which is a best practice.

Code

```
# pages/urls.py
from django.urls import path
from .views import home_page_view

urlpatterns = [
    path('', home_page_view, name='home')
]
```

The full flow of our Django homepage is as follows: * when a user goes to the homepage they will first be routed to `config/urls.py` * then routed to `pages/urls.py` * and finally directed to the `home_page_view` which returns the string "Hello, World!"

Our work is done for a basic homepage. Start up the local server again.

Command Line

```
(hello) $ python manage.py runserver
```

If you refresh the web browser at `http://127.0.0.1:8000/` it will now output our desired message.

Hello World

Now it's time to switch to Docker. Stop the local server again with `Control+c` and exit our virtual environment since we no longer need it by typing `exit`.

Command Line

```
(hello) $ exit
$
```

How do we know the virtual environment is no longer active? There will no longer be parentheses around the directory name on the command line prompt. Any normal Django commands you try to run at this point will fail. For example, try `python manage.py runserver` to see what happens.

Command Line

```
$ python manage.py runserver
File "./manage.py", line 14
  ) from exc
        ^
SyntaxError: invalid syntax
```

This means we're fully out of the virtual environment and ready for Docker.

Images, Containers, and the Docker Host

A Docker **image** is a snapshot in time of what a project contains. It is represented by a `Dockerfile` and is literally a list of instructions that must be built. A Docker **container** is a running instance of an image. To continue our apartment analogy from earlier, the image is the blueprint or set of plans for the apartment; the container is the actual, fully-built building.

The third core concept is the "Docker host" which is the underlying OS. It's possible to have multiple containers running within a single Docker host. When we refer to code or processes running *within* Docker, that means they are running in the Docker host.

Let's create our first `Dockerfile` to see all of this theory in action.

Command Line

```
$ touch Dockerfile
```

Within the `Dockerfile` add the following code which we'll walk through line-by-line below.

Dockerfile

```
# Pull base image
FROM python:3.8

# Set environment variables
ENV PYTHONDONTWRITEBYTECODE 1
ENV PYTHONUNBUFFERED 1

# Set work directory
WORKDIR /code

# Install dependencies
COPY Pipfile Pipfile.lock /code/
RUN pip install pipenv && pipenv install --system

# Copy project
COPY . /code/
```

Dockerfiles are read from top-to-bottom when an image is created. The first instruction **must** be the FROM command which lets us import a base image to use for our image, in this case Python 3.8.

Then we use the ENV command to set two environment variables:

- PYTHONUNBUFFERED ensures our console output looks familiar and is not buffered by Docker, which we don't want
- PYTHONDONTWRITEBYTECODE means Python will not try to write .pyc files which we also do not desire

Next we use WORKDIR to set a default work directory path within our image called code which is where we will store our code. If we didn't do this then each time we wanted to execute commands within our container we'd have to type in a long path. Instead Docker will just assume we mean to execute all commands from this directory.

For our dependencies we are using Pipenv so we copy over both the Pipfile and Pipfile.lock files into a /code/ directory in Docker.

It's worth taking a moment to explain why Pipenv creates a Pipfile.lock, too. The concept of lock files is not unique to Python or Pipenv; in fact it is already present in package managers for most modern programming languages: `Gemfile.lock` in Ruby, `yarn.lock` in JavaScript, `composer.lock` in PHP, and so on. `Pipenv` was the first popular project to incorporate them into Python packaging.

The benefit of a lock file is that this leads to a deterministic build: no matter how many times you install the software packages, you'll have the same result. Without a lock file that "locks down" the dependencies and their order, this is not necessarily the case. Which means that two team members who install the same list of software packages might have slightly different build installations.

When we're working with Docker where there is code both locally on our computer and also within Docker, the potential for `Pipfile.lock` conflicts arises when updating software packages. We'll explore this properly in the next chapter.

Moving along we use the `RUN` command to first install `Pipenv` and then `pipenv install` to install the software packages listed in our `Pipfile.lock`, currently just Django. It's important to add the `--system` flag as well since by default Pipenv will look for a virtual environment in which to install any package, but since we're within Docker now, technically there isn't any virtual environment. In a way, the Docker container *is* our virtual environment and more. So we must use the `--system` flag to ensure our packages are available throughout all of Docker for us.

As the final step we copy over the rest of our local code into the `/code/` directory within Docker. Why do we copy local code over twice, first the `Pipfile` and `Pipfile.lock` and then the rest? The reason is that images are created based on instructions top-down so we want things that change often–like our local code–to be last. That way we only have to regenerate that part of the image when a change happens, not reinstall everything each time there is a change. And since the software packages contained in our `Pipfile` and `Pipfile.lock` change infrequently, it makes sense to copy them over and install them earlier.

Our image instructions are now done so let's build the image using the command `docker build .` The period, `.`, indicates the current directory is where to execute the command. There will be a lot of output here; I've only included the first two lines and the last three.

Command Line

```
$ docker build .
Sending build context to Docker daemon   154.6kB
Step 1/7 : FROM python:3.8
3.8: Pulling from library/python
...
Successfully built 8d85b5d5f5f6
```

Moving on we now need to create a `docker-compose.yml` file to control how to run the container that will be built based upon our `Dockerfile` image.

Command Line

```
$ touch docker-compose.yml
```

It will contain the following code.

docker-compose.yml

```
version: '3.8'

services:
  web:
    build: .
    command: python /code/manage.py runserver 0.0.0.0:8000
    volumes:
      - .:/code
    ports:
      - 8000:8000
```

On the top line we specify the most recent version[29] of Docker Compose which is currently `3.8`. Don't be confused by the fact that Python is also on version `3.8` at the moment; there is no overlap between the two! It's just a coincidence.

Then we specify which `services` (or containers) we want to have running within our Docker host. It's possible to have multiple `services` running, but for now we just have one for `web`. We specify how to build the container by saying, Look in the current directory `.` for the `Dockerfile`. Then within the container run the `command` to start up the local server.

---

[29]https://docs.docker.com/compose/compose-file/compose-versioning/

The volumes[30] mount automatically syncs the Docker filesystem with our local computer's filesystem. This means that we don't have to rebuild the image each time we change a single file!

Lastly, we specify the ports to expose within Docker which will be 8000, which is the Django default.

If this is your first time using Docker, it is *highly likely* you are confused right now. But don't worry. We'll create multiple Docker images and containers over the course of this book and with practice the flow will start to make more sense. You'll see we use very similar Dockerfile and docker-compose.yml files in each of our projects.

The final step is to run our Docker container using the command docker-compose up. This command will result in another long stream of output code on the command line.

Command Line

```
$ docker-compose up
Creating network "hello_default" with the default driver
Building web
Step 1/7 : FROM python:3.8
...
Creating hello_web_1 ... done
Attaching to hello_web_1
web_1  | Watching for file changes with StatReloader
web_1  | Performing system checks...
web_1  |
web_1  | System check identified no issues (0 silenced).
web_1  | August 03, 2020 - 19:28:08
web_1  | Django version 3.1, using settings 'config.settings'
web_1  | Starting development server at http://0.0.0.0:8000/
web_1  | Quit the server with CONTROL-C.
```

To confirm it actually worked, go back to http://127.0.0.1:8000/ in your web browser. Refresh the page and the "Hello, World" page should still appear.

Django is now running purely within a Docker container. We are not working within a virtual environment locally. We did not execute the runserver command. All of our code now exists and our Django server is running within a self-contained Docker container. Success!

---

[30]https://docs.docker.com/storage/volumes/

Stop the container with `Control+c` (press the "Control" and "c" button at the same time) and additionally type `docker-compose down`. Docker containers take up a lot of memory so it's a good idea to stop them in this way when you're done using them. Containers are meant to be stateless which is why we use `volumes` to copy our code over locally where it can be saved.

Command Line

```
$ docker-compose down
Removing hello_web_1 ... done
Removing network hello_default
```

Git

Git[31] is the version control system of choice these days and we'll use it in this book. First add a new Git file with `git init`, then check the `status` of changes, add updates, and include a commit message.

Command Line

```
$ git init
$ git status
$ git add .
$ git commit -m 'ch1'
```

You can compare your code for this chapter with the official repository[32] available on Github.

Conclusion

Docker is a self-contained environment that includes everything we need for local development: web services, databases, and more if we want. The general pattern will always be the same when using it with Django:

- create a virtual environment locally and install Django

---

[31]https://git-scm.com/

[32]https://github.com/wsvincent/djangoforprofessionals/tree/master/ch1-hello

- create a new project
- exit the virtual environment
- write a `Dockerfile` and then build the initial image
- write a `docker-compose.yml` file and run the container with `docker-compose up`

We'll build several more Django projects with Docker so this flow makes more sense, but that's really all there is to it. In the next chapter we'll create a new Django project using Docker and add PostgreSQL in a separate container as our database.

Chapter 2: PostgreSQL

One of the most immediate differences between working on a "toy app" in Django and a production-ready one is the database. Django ships with SQLite[33] as the default choice for local development because it is small, fast, and file-based which makes it easy to use. No additional installation or configuration is required.

However this convenience comes at a cost. Generally speaking SQLite is not a good database choice for professional websites. So while it is fine to use SQLite locally while prototyping an idea, it is rare to actually use SQLite as the database on a production project.

Django ships with built-in support for four databases[34]: SQLite, PostgreSQL, MySQL, and Oracle. We'll be using PostgreSQL[35] in this book as it is the most popular choice for Django developers, however, the beauty of Django's ORM is that even if we wanted to use MySQL or Oracle, the actual Django code we write will be almost identical. The Django ORM handles the translation from Python code to the databases for us which is quite amazing if you think about it.

The challenge of using these three databases is that each must be both installed and run locally if you want to faithfully mimic a production environment on your local computer. And we do want that! While Django handles the details of switching between databases for us there are inevitably small, hard-to-catch bugs that can crop up if you use SQLite for local development but a different database in production. Therefore a best practice is use the same database locally and in production.

In this chapter we'll start a new Django project with a SQLite database and then switch over to both Docker and PostgreSQL.

---

[33]https://sqlite.org/index.html

[34]https://docs.djangoproject.com/en/3.1/ref/databases/#databases

[35]https://www.postgresql.org/

Starting

On the command line make sure you've navigated back to the code folder on our desktop. You can do this two ways. Either type cd .. to move "up" a level so if you are currently in Desktop/code/hello you will move to Desktop/code. Or you can simply type cd ~/Desktop/code/ which will take you directly to the desired directory. Then create a new directory called postgresql for this chapter's code.

Command Line

```
$ cd ..
$ mkdir postgresql && cd postgresql
```

Now install Django, start the shell, and create a basic Django project called config. Don't forget the period . at the end of the command!

Command Line

```
$ pipenv install django~=3.1.0
$ pipenv shell
(postgresql) $ django-admin startproject config .
```

So far so good. Now we can migrate our database to initialize it and use runserver to start the local server.

> Normally I don't recommend running migrate on new projects until *after* a custom user model has been configured. Otherwise Django will bind the database to the built-in User model which is difficult to modify later on in the project. We'll cover this properly in Chapter 3 but since this chapter is primarily for demonstration purposes, using the default User model here is a one-time exception.

Command Line

```
(postgresql) $ python manage.py migrate
(postgresql) $ python manage.py runserver
```

Confirm everything worked by navigating to `http://127.0.0.1:8000/` in your web browser. You may need to refresh the page but should see the familiar Django welcome page.

Stop the local server with `Control+c` and then use the `ls` command to list all files and directories.

Command Line

```
(postresql) $ ls
Pipfile        Pipfile.lock        config        db.sqlite3        manage.py
```

Docker

To switch over to Docker first `exit` our virtual environment and then create `Dockerfile` and `docker-compose.yml` files which will control our Docker image and container respectively.

Command Line

```
(postgresql) $ exit
$ touch Dockerfile
$ touch docker-compose.yml
```

The `Dockerfile` is the same as in Chapter 1.

Dockerfile

```
# Pull base image
FROM python:3.8

# Set environment variables
ENV PYTHONDONTWRITEBYTECODE 1
ENV PYTHONUNBUFFERED 1

# Set work directory
WORKDIR /code

# Install dependencies
COPY Pipfile Pipfile.lock /code/
RUN pip install pipenv && pipenv install --system

# Copy project
COPY . /code/
```

Go ahead and build the initial image now using the `docker build .` command.

Command Line

```
$ docker build .
```

Did you notice that the `Dockerfile` built an image much faster this time around? That's because Docker looks locally on your computer first for a specific image. If it doesn't find an image locally it will then download it. And since many of these images were already on the computer from the previous chapter, Docker didn't need to download them all again!

Time now for the `docker-compose.yml` file which also matches what we saw previously in Chapter 1.

docker-compose.yml

```
version: '3.8'

services:
  web:
    build: .
    command: python /code/manage.py runserver 0.0.0.0:8000
    volumes:
      - .:/code
    ports:
      - 8000:8000
```

Detached Mode

We'll start up our container now but this time in detached mode which requires either the `-d` or `-detach` flag (they do the same thing).

Command Line

```
$ docker-compose up -d
```

Detached mode runs containers in the background[36], which means we can use a single command line tab without needing a separate one open as well. This saves us from switching back and forth between two command line tabs constantly. The downside is that if/when there is an error, the output won't always be visible. So if your screen does not match this book at some point, try typing `docker-compose logs` to see the current output and debug any issues.

You likely will see a "Warning: Image for service web was built because it did not already exist" message at the bottom of the command. Docker automatically created a new image for us within the container. As we'll see later in the book, adding the `--build` flag to force an image build is necessary when software packages are updated because, by default, Docker will look for a local cached copy of software and use that which improves performance.

To confirm things are working properly go back to `http://127.0.0.1:8000/` in your web browser. Refresh the page to see the Django welcome page again.

---

[36]https://docs.docker.com/compose/reference/up/

Since we're working *within Docker* now as opposed to locally we must preface traditional commands with `docker-compose exec [service]` where we specify the name of the service. For example, to create a superuser account instead of typing `python manage.py createsuperuser` the updated command would now look like the line below, using the `web` service.

Command Line

```
$ docker-compose exec web python manage.py createsuperuser
```

For the username choose `sqliteadmin`, `sqliteadmin@email.com` as the email address, and select the password of your choice. I often use `testpass123`.

Then navigate directly into the admin at `http://127.0.0.1:8000/admin` and log in. You will be redirected to the admin homepage. Note in the upper right corner `sqliteadmin` is the username.

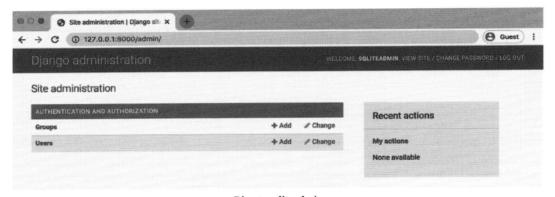

Django sqliteadmin

If you click on the `Users` button it takes us to the Users page where we can confirm only one user has been created.

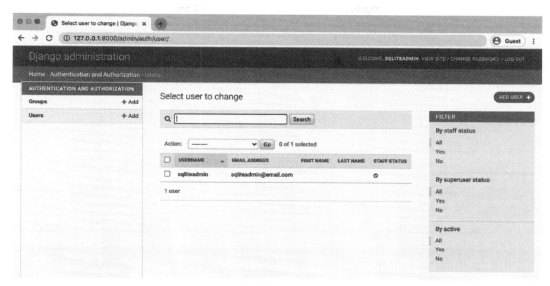

Admin Users page

It's important to highlight another aspect of Docker at this point: so far we've been updating our database-currently represented by the `db.sqlite3` file-within Docker. That means the actual `db.sqlite3` file is changing each time. And thanks to the `volumes` mount in our `docker-compose.yml` config each file change has been copied over into a `db.sqlite3` file on our local computer too. You could quit Docker, start the `shell`, start the server with `python manage.py runserver`, and see the exact same admin login at this point because the underlying SQLite database is the same.

PostgreSQL

Now it's time to switch over to PostgreSQL for our project which takes three additional steps:

- install a database adapter, `psycopg2`, so Python can talk to PostgreSQL
- update the `DATABASE` config in our `settings.py` file
- install and run PostgreSQL locally

Ready? Here we go. Stop the running Docker container with `docker-compose down`.

Command Line

```
$ docker-compose down
Stopping postgresql_d_1 ... done
Removing postgresql_web_1 ... done
Removing network postgresql_default
```

Then within our `docker-compose.yml` file add a new service called `db`. This means there will be two separate services, each a container, running within our Docker host: `web` for the Django local server and `db` for our PostgreSQL database.

The PostgreSQL version will be pinned to the latest version, `11`. If we had not specified a version number and instead used just `postgres`, then the latest version of PostgreSQL would be downloaded, even if that version in the future is 12, 13, or another number. It's always good to pin to a specific version number, both for databases and packages.

The second part is adding the `environment` variable setting for `POSTGRES_HOST_AUTH_METHOD=trust`, which allows us to connect without a password. This is a convenience for local development.

Finally, we add a `depends_on` line to our `web` service since it literally depends on the database to run. This means that `db` will be started up before `web`.

docker-compose.yml

```
version: '3.8'

services:
  web:
    build: .
    command: python /code/manage.py runserver 0.0.0.0:8000
    volumes:
      - .:/code
    ports:
      - 8000:8000
    depends_on:
      - db
  db:
    image: postgres:11
    environment:
      - "POSTGRES_HOST_AUTH_METHOD=trust"
```

Now run `docker-compose up -d` which will rebuild our image and spin up two containers, one running PostgreSQL within `db` and the other our Django `web` server.

Command Line

```
$ docker-compose up -d
```

It's important to note at this point that a production database like PostgreSQL is not file-based. It runs entirely within the `db` service and is ephemeral; when we execute `docker-compose down` all data within it will be lost. This is in contrast to our code in the `web` container which has a `volumes` mount to sync local and Docker code.

In the next chapter we'll learn how to add a `volumes` mount for our `db` service to persist our database information.

Settings

With your text editor, open the `config/settings.py` file and scroll down to the `DATABASES` config. The current setting is this:

Code

```python
# config/settings.py
DATABASES = {
    'default': {
        'ENGINE': 'django.db.backends.sqlite3',
        'NAME': BASE_DIR / 'db.sqlite3',
    }
}
```

By default Django specifies `sqlite3` as the database engine, gives it the name `db.sqlite3`, and places it at `BASE_DIR` which means in our project-level directory.

Since directory structure is often a point of confusion "project-level" means the top directory of our project which contains `config`, `manage.py`, `Pipfile`, `Pipfile.lock`, and the `db.slite3` file.

Command Line

```
(postgresql) $ ls
Dockerfile    Pipfile.lock    docker-compose.yml    config
Pipfile    db.sqlite3    manage.py
```

To switch over to PostgreSQL we will update the ENGINE[37] configuration. PostgreSQL requires a NAME, USER, PASSWORD, HOST, and PORT.

For convenience we'll set the first three to postgres, the HOST to db which is the name of our service set in docker-compose.yml, and the PORT to 5432 which is the default PostgreSQL port[38].

Code

```
# config/settings.py
DATABASES = {
    'default': {
        'ENGINE': 'django.db.backends.postgresql',
        'NAME': 'postgres',
        'USER': 'postgres',
        'PASSWORD': 'postgres',
        'HOST': 'db',
        'PORT': 5432
    }
}
```

You will see an error now if your refresh the web page at http://127.0.0.1:8000/.

---

[37] https://docs.djangoproject.com/en/3.1/ref/settings/#std:setting-DATABASE-ENGINE
[38] https://en.wikipedia.org/wiki/Port_%28computer_networking%29

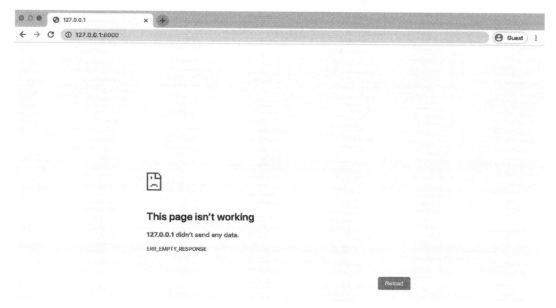

Django error

What's happening? Since we're running Docker in detached mode with the -d flag it's not immediately clear. Time to check our logs.

Command Line

```
$ docker-compose logs
...
web_1  | django.core.exceptions.ImproperlyConfigured: Error loading psycopg2
module: No module named 'psycopg2'
```

There will be a lot of output but at the bottom of the web_1 section you'll see the above lines which tells us we haven't installed the psycopg2 driver yet.

Psycopg

PostgreSQL is a database that can be used by almost any programming language. But if you think about it, how does a programming language–and they all vary in some way or another–connect to the database itself?

The answer is via a database adapter! And that's what Psycopg[39] is, the most popular database adapter for Python. If you'd like to learn more about how Psycopg works here is a link to a fuller description[40] on the official site.

We can install Pyscopg with Pipenv. On the command line, enter the following command so it is installed within our Docker host.

Command Line

```
$ docker-compose exec web pipenv install psycopg2-binary==2.8.5
```

Why install within Docker rather than locally I hope you're asking? The short answer is that consistently installing new software packages within Docker and then rebuilding the image from scratch will save us from potential `Pipfile.lock` conflicts.

The `Pipfile.lock` generation depends heavily on the OS being used. We've specified our entire OS within Docker, including using `Python 3.8`. But if you install `psycopg2` locally on your computer, which has a different environment, the resulting `Pipfile.lock` file will also be different. But then the `volumes` mount in our `docker-compose.yml` file, which automatically syncs the local and Docker filesystems, will cause the local `Pipfile.lock` to overwrite the version within Docker. So now our Docker container is trying to run an incorrect `Pipfile.lock` file. Ack!

One way to avoid these issues is to consistently install new software packages within Docker rather than locally.

If you now refresh the webpage you will....still see an error. Ok, let's check the logs.

Command Line

```
$ docker-compose logs
```

It's the same as before! Why does this happen? Docker automatically caches images unless something changes for performance reasons. We want it to automatically rebuild the image with our new `Pipfile` and `Pipfile.lock` but because the last line of our `Dockerfile` is COPY . /code/

---

[39]http://initd.org/psycopg/
[40]http://initd.org/psycopg/docs/index.html

only the files will copy; the underlying image won't rebuild itself unless we force it too. This can be done by adding the `--build` flag.

So to review: whenever adding a new package first install it within Docker, stop the containers, force an image rebuild, and then start the containers up again. We'll use this flow repeatedly throughout the book.

Command Line

```
$ docker-compose down
$ docker-compose up -d --build
```

If you refresh the homepage again the Django welcome page at `http://127.0.0.1:8000/` now works! That's because Django has successfully connected to PostgreSQL via Docker.

Great, everything is working.

New Database

However, since we are using PostgreSQL now, not SQLite, our database is empty. If you look at the current logs again by typing `docker-compose logs` you'll see complaints like "You have 18 unapplied migrations(s)".

To reinforce this point visit the Admin at `http://127.0.0.1:8000/admin/` and log in. Will our previous superuser account of `sqliteadmin` and `testpass123` work?

Nope! We see `ProgrammingError at /admin`. To fix this situation, we can both migrate and create a superuser *within* Docker that will access the PostgreSQL database.

Command Line

```
$ docker-compose exec web python manage.py migrate
$ docker-compose exec web python manage.py createsuperuser
```

What should we call our superuser? Let's use `postgresqladmin` and for testing purposes set the email to `postgresqladmin@email.com` and the password to `testpass123`.

In your web browser navigate to the admin page at `http://127.0.0.1:8000/admin/` and enter in the new superuser log in information.

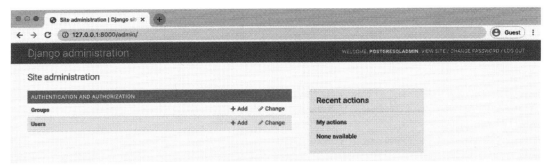

Admin with postgresadmin

In the upper right corner it shows that we are logged in with `postgresadmin` now not `sqliteadmin`. Also, you can click on the `Users` tab on the homepage and visit the Users section to see our one and only user is the new superuser account.

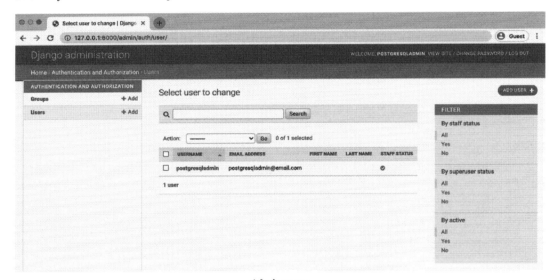

Admin users

Remember to stop our running container with `docker-compose down`.

Command Line

```
$ docker-compose down
```

Git

Let's save our changes again by initializing Git for this new project, adding our changes, and including a commit message.

Command Line

```
$ git init
$ git status
$ git add .
$ git commit -m 'ch2'
```

The official source code for Chapter 2 is available on Github[41].

Conclusion

The goal of this chapter was to demonstrate how Docker and PostgreSQL work together on a Django project. Switching between a SQLite database and a PostgreSQL is a mental leap for many developers initially.

The key point is that with Docker we don't need to be in a local virtual environment anymore. Docker is our virtual environment...and our database and more if desired. The Docker host essentially replaces our local operating system and within it we can run multiple containers, such as for our web app and for our database, which can all be isolated and run separately.

In the next chapter we will start our online Bookstore project. Let's begin!

---

[41]https://github.com/wsvincent/djangoforprofessionals/tree/master/ch2-postgresql

Chapter 3: Bookstore Project

It is time to build the main project of this book, an online Bookstore. In this chapter we will start a new project, switch over to Docker, add a custom user model, and implement our first tests.

Let's start by creating a new Django project with Pipenv locally and then switch over to Docker. You're likely in the postgresql directory right now from Chapter 2 so on the command line type cd .. which will take you back to the desired code directory on the Desktop (assuming you're on a Mac). We'll create a books directory for our code, and then install django. We also know we'll be using PostgreSQL so we can install the psycopg2 adapter now too. It is only *after* we have built our initial image that we start installing future software packages within Docker itself. Lastly use the shell command to enter the new virtual environment.

Command Line

```
$ cd ..
$ mkdir books && cd books
$ pipenv install django~=3.1.0 psycopg2-binary==2.8.5
$ pipenv shell
```

We'll name our new Django project config. Make sure you don't forget that period, ., at the end of the command or else Django will create an extra directory which we don't need. Then use runserver to start the local Django web server and confirm everything is working correctly.

Command Line

```
(books) $ django-admin startproject config .
(books) $ python manage.py runserver
```

In your web browser go to http://127.0.0.1:8000/ and you should see the friendly Django welcome page.

Django welcome page

On the command line you will likely see a warning about "18 unapplied migration(s)". It's safe to ignore this for now since we're about to switch over to Docker and PostgreSQL.

Docker

We can now switch over to Docker in our project. Go ahead and stop the local server `Control+c` and also exit the virtual environment shell.

Command Line

```
(books) $ exit
$
```

Docker should already be installed and the desktop app running from the previous chapter. Per usual we need to create a `Dockerfile` and `docker-compose.yml` file.

Command Line

```
$ touch Dockerfile
$ touch docker-compose.yml
```

The `Dockerfile` will be the same as before.

Dockerfile

```
# Pull base image
FROM python:3.8

# Set environment variables
ENV PYTHONDONTWRITEBYTECODE 1
ENV PYTHONUNBUFFERED 1

# Set work directory
WORKDIR /code

# Install dependencies
COPY Pipfile Pipfile.lock /code/
RUN pip install pipenv && pipenv install --system

# Copy project
COPY . /code/
```

Docker containers are, by their nature, ephemeral. They only exist when being run and all data within them is deleted when the container stops. We work around this by using `volumes` for persistent data. Within the web service we already have a volume that links our local code to the running container and vice versa. But we don't have a dedicated volume for our PostgreSQL database, so any information in there will be lost when the container stops running. The solution is to add a volume for the database, too. We do this by specifying a location for volumes within the db service and then also a volumes that lives outside of the containers.

This is likely quite confusing and a full explanation is beyond the scope of this book as it's focused on Django, not Docker. However the takeaway is that Docker containers do not store persistent data so anything we want to keep like source code or database information, must have a dedicated volume or else it will be lost each time a container is stopped. You can read the Docker documentation on volumes[42] for a more technical explanation of how this all works if you're interested.

In any event, here is the updated code for our docker-compose.yml file that supports a database volume now.

docker-compose.yml

```
version: '3.8'

services:
  web:
    build: .
    command: python /code/manage.py runserver 0.0.0.0:8000
    volumes:
      - .:/code
    ports:
      - 8000:8000
    depends_on:
      - db
  db:
    image: postgres:11
    volumes:
      - postgres_data:/var/lib/postgresql/data/
    environment:
      - "POSTGRES_HOST_AUTH_METHOD=trust"

volumes:
  postgres_data:
```

---

[42]https://docs.docker.com/storage/volumes/

We can build our image and run the containers with one command.

Command Line

```
$ docker-compose up -d --build
```

> If you see an error here like `Bindfor 0.0.0.0:8000 failed: port is already allocated`
> then you did not fully stop the Docker container from Chapter 2. Try running `docker-compose`
> `down` in the directory where you previously ran it, probably `postgresql`. Then attempt to build
> and run our new image and container again. If that approach *still* fails you can quit the Docker
> desktop application completely and then open it again.

Go to the web browser now at `http://127.0.0.1:8000/` and click refresh. It should be the same
friendly Django welcome page albeit now running inside of Docker.

PostgreSQL

Even though we already installed `psycopg` and have PostgreSQL available in our `docker-compose.yml`
file we still must direct Django to switch over to it instead of the default SQLite database. Do that
now. The code is the same as in the previous chapter.

Code

```
# config/settings.py
DATABASES = {
    'default': {
        'ENGINE': 'django.db.backends.postgresql',
        'NAME': 'postgres',
        'USER': 'postgres',
        'PASSWORD': 'postgres',
        'HOST': 'db',
        'PORT': 5432
    }
}
```

Refresh the web browser for the homepage to confirm everything still works correctly.

Custom User Model

Time to implement a custom user model which the official Django documentation "highly recommends."[43] Why? Because you *will* need to make changes to the built-in User model at some point in your project's life.

If you have not started with a custom user model from the very first migrate command you run, then you're in for a world of hurt because User is tightly interwoven with the rest of Django internally. It is challenging to switch over to a custom user model mid-project.

A point of confusion for many people is that custom user models were only added in Django 1.5. Up until that point the recommended approach was to add a OneToOneField[44], often called a Profile model, to User. You'll often see this set up in older projects.

But these days using a custom user model is the more common approach. However as with many things Django-related, there are implementation choices: either extend AbstractUser[45] which keeps the default User fields and permissions or extend AbstractBaseUser[46] which is even more granular, and flexible, but requires more work.

We'll stick with the simpler AbstractUser in this book as AbstractBaseUser can be added later if needed.

There are four steps for adding a custom user model to our project:

1. Create a CustomUser model
2. Update config/settings.py
3. Customize UserCreationForm and UserChangeForm
4. Add the custom user model to admin.py

The first step is to create a CustomUser model which will live within its own app. I like to name this app accounts. We could do this either locally within our virtual environment shell, meaning we'd

---

[43]https://docs.djangoproject.com/en/3.1/topics/auth/customizing/#using-a-custom-user-model-when-starting-a-project

[44]https://docs.djangoproject.com/en/3.1/ref/models/fields/#django.db.models.OneToOneField

[45]https://docs.djangoproject.com/en/3.1/topics/auth/customizing/#django.contrib.auth.models.AbstractUser

[46]https://docs.djangoproject.com/en/3.1/topics/auth/customizing/#django.contrib.auth.models.AbstractBaseUser

go `pipenv shell` and then run `python manage.py startapp accounts`. However for consistency we'll run the majority of our commands within Docker itself.

Command Line

```
$ docker-compose exec web python manage.py startapp accounts
```

Create a new `CustomUser` model which extends `AbstractUser`. That means we're essentially making a copy where `CustomUser` now has inherited all the functionality of `AbstractUser`, but we can override or add new functionality as needed. We're not making any changes yet so include the Python `pass` statement which acts as a placeholder for our future code.

Code

```
# accounts/models.py
from django.contrib.auth.models import AbstractUser
from django.db import models


class CustomUser(AbstractUser):
    pass
```

Now go in and update our `settings.py` file in the `INSTALLED_APPS` section to tell Django about our new accounts app. We also want to add a `AUTH_USER_MODEL` config at the bottom of the file which will cause our project to use `CustomUser` instead of the default `User` model.

Code

```
# config/settings.py
INSTALLED_APPS = [
    'django.contrib.admin',
    'django.contrib.auth',
    'django.contrib.contenttypes',
    'django.contrib.sessions',
    'django.contrib.messages',
    'django.contrib.staticfiles',

    # Local
    'accounts', # new
]
...
AUTH_USER_MODEL = 'accounts.CustomUser' # new
```

Time to create a migrations file for the changes. We'll add the optional app name `accounts` to the command so that only changes to that app are included.

Command Line

```
$ docker-compose exec web python manage.py makemigrations accounts
Migrations for 'accounts':
  accounts/migrations/0001_initial.py
    - Create model CustomUser
```

Then run `migrate` to initialize the database for the very first time.

Command Line

```
$ docker-compose exec web python manage.py migrate
```

Custom User Forms

A user model can be both created and edited within the Django admin. So we'll need to update the built-in forms too to point to `CustomUser` instead of `User`.

Create a `accounts/forms.py` file.

Command Line

```
$ touch accounts/forms.py
```

In your text editor type in the following code to switch over to `CustomUser`.

Code

```python
# accounts/forms.py
from django.contrib.auth import get_user_model
from django.contrib.auth.forms import UserCreationForm, UserChangeForm


class CustomUserCreationForm(UserCreationForm):

    class Meta:
        model = get_user_model()
        fields = ('email', 'username',)


class CustomUserChangeForm(UserChangeForm):

    class Meta:
        model = get_user_model()
        fields = ('email', 'username',)
```

At the very top we've imported `CustomUser` model via get_user_model[47] which looks to our `AUTH_USER_MODEL` config in `settings.py`. This might feel a bit more circular than directly importing `CustomUser` here, but it enforces the idea of making one single reference to the custom user model rather than directly referring to it all over our project.

Next we import UserCreationForm[48] and UserChangeForm[49] which will both be extended.

Then create two new forms–`CustomUserCreationForm` and `CustomUserChangeForm`–that extend the base user forms imported above and specify swapping in our `CustomUser` model and displaying the fields `email` and `username`. The `password` field is implicitly included by default and so does not need to be explicitly named here as well.

Custom User Admin

Finally we have to update our `accounts/admin.py` file. The admin is a common place to manipulate user data and there is tight coupling between the built-in `User` and the admin.

---

[47]https://docs.djangoproject.com/en/3.1/topics/auth/customizing/#django.contrib.auth.get_user_model
[48]https://docs.djangoproject.com/en/3.1/topics/auth/default/#django.contrib.auth.forms.UserCreationForm
[49]https://docs.djangoproject.com/en/3.1/topics/auth/default/#django.contrib.auth.forms.UserChangeForm

We'll extend the existing `UserAdmin` into `CustomUserAdmin` and tell Django to use our new forms, custom user model, and list only the email and username of a user. If we wanted to we could add more of the existing `User` fields[50] to `list_display` such as `is_staff`.

Code

```
# accounts/admin.py
from django.contrib import admin
from django.contrib.auth import get_user_model
from django.contrib.auth.admin import UserAdmin

from .forms import CustomUserCreationForm, CustomUserChangeForm

CustomUser = get_user_model()


class CustomUserAdmin(UserAdmin):
    add_form = CustomUserCreationForm
    form = CustomUserChangeForm
    model = CustomUser
    list_display = ['email', 'username',]

admin.site.register(CustomUser, CustomUserAdmin)
```

Phew. A bit of code upfront but this saves a ton of heartache later on.

Superuser

A good way to confirm our custom user model is up and running properly is to create a superuser account so we can log into the admin. This command will access `CustomUserCreationForm` under the hood.

Command Line

```
$ docker-compose exec web python manage.py createsuperuser
```

I've used the username `wsv`, email of `will@learndjango.com`, and password `testpass123`. You can use your own preferred variations here.

---

[50]https://docs.djangoproject.com/en/3.1/ref/contrib/auth/

Now go to `http://127.0.0.1:8000/admin` and confirm that you can log in. You should see your superuser name in the upper right corner on the post-log in page.

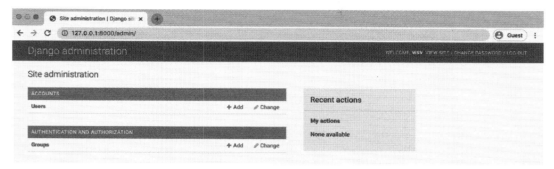

Django admin homepage

You can also click on the `Users` section to see the email and username of your superuser account.

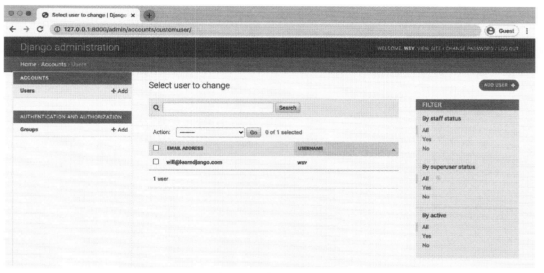

Django admin users page

Tests

Since we've added new functionality to our project we should test it. Whether you are a solo developer or working on a team, tests are important. In the words of Django co-founder Jacob

Kaplan-Moss, "Code without tests is broken as designed."

There are two main types of tests:

- *Unit tests* are small, fast, and isolated to a specific piece of functionality
- *Integration tests* are large, slow, and used for testing an entire application or a user flow like payment that covers multiple screens

You should write many unit tests and a small number of integration tests.

The Python programming language contains its own unit testing framework[51] and Django's automated testing framework[52] extends this with multiple additions into a web context. There is no excuse for not writing a lot of tests; they will save you time.

It's important to note that not everything needs to be tested. For example, any built-in Django features already contain tests in the source code. If we were using the default `User` model in our project we would not need to test it. But since we've created a `CustomUser` model we should.

Unit Tests

To write unit tests in Django we use TestCase[53] which is, itself, an extension of Python's TestCase[54]. Our `accounts` app already contains a `tests.py` file which is automatically added when the `startapp` command is used. Currently it is blank. Let's fix that!

Each method must be prefaced with `test` in order to be run by the Django test suite. It is also a good idea to be overly descriptive with your unit test names since mature projects have hundreds if not thousands of tests!

---

[51]https://docs.python.org/3/library/unittest.html

[52]https://docs.djangoproject.com/en/3.1/topics/testing/

[53]https://docs.djangoproject.com/en/3.1/topics/testing/tools/#django.test.TestCase

[54]https://docs.python.org/3/library/unittest.html#unittest.TestCase

Code

```
# accounts/tests.py
from django.contrib.auth import get_user_model
from django.test import TestCase


class CustomUserTests(TestCase):

    def test_create_user(self):
        User = get_user_model()
        user = User.objects.create_user(
            username='will',
            email='will@email.com',
            password='testpass123'
        )
        self.assertEqual(user.username, 'will')
        self.assertEqual(user.email, 'will@email.com')
        self.assertTrue(user.is_active)
        self.assertFalse(user.is_staff)
        self.assertFalse(user.is_superuser)

    def test_create_superuser(self):
        User = get_user_model()
        admin_user = User.objects.create_superuser(
            username='superadmin',
            email='superadmin@email.com',
            password='testpass123'
        )
        self.assertEqual(admin_user.username, 'superadmin')
        self.assertEqual(admin_user.email, 'superadmin@email.com')
        self.assertTrue(admin_user.is_active)
        self.assertTrue(admin_user.is_staff)
        self.assertTrue(admin_user.is_superuser)
```

We have imported both `get_user_model` and `TestCase` before creating a `CustomUserTests` class. Within it are two separate tests. `test_create_user` confirms that a new user can be created. First we set our user model to the variable `User` and then create one via the manager method `create_user`[55] which does the actual work of creating a new user with the proper permissions.

---

[55]https://docs.djangoproject.com/en/3.1/ref/contrib/auth/#django.contrib.auth.models.UserManager.create_user

For `test_create_superuser` we follow a similar pattern but reference create_superuser[56] instead of `create_user`. The difference between the two users is that a superuser should have both `is_staff` and `is_superuser` set to True.

To run our tests within Docker we'll prefix `docker-compose exec web` to the traditional command `python manage.py test`.

Command Line

```
$ docker-compose exec web python manage.py test
Creating test database for alias 'default'...
System check identified no issues (0 silenced).
..
----------------------------------------------------------------
Ran 2 tests in 0.268s

OK
Destroying test database for alias 'default'...
```

All the tests pass so we can proceed.

Git

We've accomplished quite a lot in this chapter so it is a good point to pause and commit our work by initializing a new Git repository, adding changes, and including a commit message.

Command Line

```
$ git init
$ git status
$ git add .
$ git commit -m 'ch3'
```

You can compare with the official source code for this chapter on Github[57].

---

[56]https://docs.djangoproject.com/en/3.1/ref/contrib/auth/#django.contrib.auth.models.UserManager.create_superuser

[57]https://github.com/wsvincent/djangoforprofessionals/tree/master/ch3-books

Conclusion

Our Bookstore project is now running with Docker and PostgreSQL and we've configured a custom user model. Next up will be a `pages` app for our static pages.

Chapter 4: Pages App

Let's build a homepage for our new project. For now this will be a static page meaning it will not interact with the database in any way. Later on it will be a dynamic page displaying books for sale but... one thing at a time.

It's common to have multiple static pages in even a mature project such as an About page so let's create a dedicated pages app for them.

On the command line use the startapp command again to make a pages app.

Command Line

```
$ docker-compose exec web python manage.py startapp pages
```

Then add it to our INSTALLED_APPS setting. We'll also update TEMPLATES so that Django will look for a project-level templates folder. By default Django looks within each app for a templates folder, but organizing all templates in one space is easier to manage.

Code

```python
# config/settings.py
INSTALLED_APPS = [
    'django.contrib.admin',
    'django.contrib.auth',
    'django.contrib.contenttypes',
    'django.contrib.sessions',
    'django.contrib.messages',
    'django.contrib.staticfiles',

    # Local
    'accounts',
    'pages', # new
]

TEMPLATES = [
    {
        ...
```

```
        'DIRS': [str(BASE_DIR.joinpath('templates'))], # new
        ...
    }
]
```

> Note that updating the DIRS setting means that Django will *also* look in this new folder; it will
> still look for any templates folders within an app.

Templates

Moving on it's time to create that new templates directory and put two files within it: _base.html
and home.html. The first base level file will be inherited by all other files; home.html will be our
homepage.

Command Line

```
$ mkdir templates
$ touch templates/_base.html
$ touch templates/home.html
```

> Why call the base template _base.html with the underscore instead of base.html? This is
> optional, but some developers prefer to add an underscore _ to denote a file that is intended
> to be inherited by other files and not displayed on its own.

In the base file we'll include the bare minimum needed and add block tags for both title and
content. Block tags give higher-level templates the option to override just the content within the
tags. For example, the homepage will have a title of "Home" but we want that to appear between
html <title></title> tags. Using block tags make it easier to update this content, as needed, in
inherited templates.

Why use the name `content` for the main content of our project? This name could be anything—`main` or some other generic indicator—but using `content` is a common naming convention in the Django world. Can you use something else? Absolutely. Is `content` the most common one you'll see? Yes.

Code

```
<!-- templates/_base.html -->
<!DOCTYPE html>
<html>
<head>
  <meta charset="utf-8">
  <title>{% block title %}Bookstore{% endblock title %}</title>
</head>
<body>
  <div class="container">
    {% block content %}
    {% endblock content %}
  </div>
</body>
</html>
```

Now for the homepage which will simply say "Homepage" for now.

Code

```
<!-- templates/home.html -->
{% extends '_base.html' %}

{% block title %}Home{% endblock title %}

{% block content %}
  <h1>Homepage</h1>
{% endblock content %}
```

URLs and Views

Every webpage in our Django project needs a `urls.py` and `views.py` file to go along with the template. For beginners the fact that order doesn't really matter here—we need all 3 files and really often a 4th, `models.py`, for the database–is confusing. Generally I prefer to start with the urls and work from there but there is no "right way" to build out this connected web of Django files.

Let's start with our project-level `urls.py` to set the proper path for webpages within the `pages` app. Since we want to create a homepage we add no additional prefix to the URL route which is designated by the empty string `''`. We also import `include` on the second line to concisely add the `pages` app to our main `urls.py` file.

Code

```
# config/urls.py
from django.contrib import admin
from django.urls import path, include # new

urlpatterns = [
    path('admin/', admin.site.urls),
    path('', include('pages.urls')), # new
]
```

Next we create a `urls.py` file within the `pages` app.

Command Line

```
$ touch pages/urls.py
```

This file will import the `HomePageView` and set the path, again, to the empty string `''`. Note that we provide an optional, but recommended, named URL[58] of `'home'` at the end. This will come in handy shortly.

---

[58]https://docs.djangoproject.com/en/3.1/topics/http/urls/#naming-url-patterns

Code

```
# pages/urls.py
from django.urls import path
from .views import HomePageView

urlpatterns = [
    path('', HomePageView.as_view(), name='home'),
]
```

Finally we need a `views.py` file. We can leverage Django's built-in TemplateView[59] so that the only tweak needed is to specify our desired template, `home.html`.

Code

```
# pages/views.py
from django.views.generic import TemplateView


class HomePageView(TemplateView):
    template_name = 'home.html'
```

We're *almost* done. If you navigate to the homepage now at `http://127.0.0.1:8000/` you'll actually see an error. But what's causing it? Since we're running the container in background detached mode–that `-d` flag–we must explicitly check the logs to see console output.

So type `docker-compose logs` which will turn up an error "ModuleNotFoundError: No module named 'pages.urls'". What's happening is that Django does not automatically update the `settings.py` file for us based on a change. In a non-Docker world stopping and restarting the server does the trick. We must do the same here which means typing `docker-compose down` and then `docker-compose up -d` to load the new `books` app in properly.

---

[59]https://docs.djangoproject.com/en/3.1/ref/class-based-views/base/#django.views.generic.base.
TemplateView

Command Line

```
$ docker-compose down
$ docker-compose up -d
```

Refresh the homepage now and it will work.

Homepage

Tests

Time for tests. For our homepage we can use Django's SimpleTestCase[60] which is a special subset of Django's `TestCase` that is designed for webpages that do not have a model included.

Testing can feel overwhelming at first, but it quickly becomes a bit boring. You'll use the same structure and techniques over and over again. In your text editor, update the existing `pages/tests.py` file. We'll start by testing the template.

Code

```
# pages/tests.py
from django.test import SimpleTestCase
from django.urls import reverse


class HomepageTests(SimpleTestCase):

    def test_homepage_status_code(self):
        response = self.client.get('/')
        self.assertEqual(response.status_code, 200)

    def test_homepage_url_name(self):
        response = self.client.get(reverse('home'))
        self.assertEqual(response.status_code, 200)
```

---

[60]https://docs.djangoproject.com/en/3.1/topics/testing/tools/#simpletestcase

At the top we import `SimpleTestCase` as well as reverse[61] which is useful for testing our URLs. Then we create a class called `HomepageTests` that extends `SimpleTestCase` and within it add a method for each unit test.

Note that we're adding `self` as the first argument of each unit test. This is a Python convention[62] that is worth repeating.

It is best to be overly descriptive with your unit test names but be aware that each method must start with `test` to be run by the Django test suite.

The two tests here both check that the HTTP status code for the homepage equals `200` which means that it exists. It does not yet tell us anything specific about the contents of the page. For `test_homepageview_status_code` we're creating a variable called `response` that accesses the homepage (/) and then uses Python's assertEqual[63] to check that the status code matches 200. A similar pattern exists for `test_homepage_url_name` except that we are calling the URL name of `home` via the `reverse` method. Recall that we added this to the `pages/urls.py` file as a best practice. Even if we change the actual route of this page in the future, we can still refer to it by the same `home` URL name.

To run our tests execute the command prefaced with `docker-compose exec web` so that it runs within Docker itself.

Command Line

```
$ docker-compose exec web python manage.py test
Creating test database for alias 'default'...
System check identified no issues (0 silenced).
..
----------------------------------------------------------------
Ran 4 tests in 0.277s

OK
Destroying test database for alias 'default'...
```

Why does it say 4 tests when we only created 2? Because we're testing the entire Django project and in the previous chapter under `users/tests.py` we added two tests for the custom user

---

[61]https://docs.djangoproject.com/en/3.1/ref/urlresolvers/#reverse

[62]https://docs.python.org/3/tutorial/classes.html#random-remarks

[63]https://docs.python.org/3/library/unittest.html#unittest.TestCase.assertEqual

model. If we wanted to only run tests for the `pages` app we simply append that name onto the command so `docker-compose exec web python manage.py test pages`.

Testing Templates

So far we've tested that the homepage exists, but we should also confirm that it uses the correct template. `SimpleTestCase` comes with a method assertTemplateUsed[64] just for this purpose! Let's use it.

Code

```
# pages/tests.py
from django.test import SimpleTestCase
from django.urls import reverse


class HomepageTests(SimpleTestCase):

    def test_homepage_status_code(self):
        response = self.client.get('/')
        self.assertEqual(response.status_code, 200)

    def test_homepage_url_name(self):
        response = self.client.get(reverse('home'))
        self.assertEqual(response.status_code, 200)

    def test_homepage_template(self): # new
        response = self.client.get('/')
        self.assertTemplateUsed(response, 'home.html')
```

We've created a `response` variable again and then checked that the template `home.html` is used. Let's run the tests again.

---

[64]https://docs.djangoproject.com/en/3.1/topics/testing/tools/#django.test.SimpleTestCase. assertTemplateUsed

Command Line

```
$ docker-compose exec web python manage.py test pages
Creating test database for alias 'default'...
System check identified no issues (0 silenced).
...
------------------------------------------------------------------
Ran 3 tests in 0.023s

OK
Destroying test database for alias 'default'...
```

Did you notice something different in that command? We added the name of our app pages so that *only* the tests within that app were run. At this early state it's fine to run all the tests, but in larger projects if you know that you've only added tests within a specific app, it can save time to just run the updated/new tests and not the entire suite.

Testing HTML

Let's now confirm that our homepage has the correct HTML code and also does not have incorrect text. It's always good to test both that tests pass and that tests we expect to fail do, actually, fail!

Code

```python
# pages/tests.py
from django.test import SimpleTestCase
from django.urls import reverse, resolve
from .views import HomePageView


class HomepageTests(SimpleTestCase):

    def test_homepage_status_code(self):
        response = self.client.get('/')
        self.assertEqual(response.status_code, 200)

    def test_homepage_url_name(self):
        response = self.client.get(reverse('home'))
        self.assertEqual(response.status_code, 200)
```

```
    def test_homepage_template(self):
        response = self.client.get('/')
        self.assertTemplateUsed(response, 'home.html')

    def test_homepage_contains_correct_html(self): # new
        response = self.client.get('/')
        self.assertContains(response, 'Homepage')

    def test_homepage_does_not_contain_incorrect_html(self): # new
        response = self.client.get('/')
        self.assertNotContains(
            response, 'Hi there! I should not be on the page.')
```

Run the tests again.

Command Line

```
$ docker-compose exec web python manage.py test
Creating test database for alias 'default'...
System check identified no issues (0 silenced).
.....
----------------------------------------------------------------------
Ran 7 tests in 0.279s

OK
Destroying test database for alias 'default'...
```

setUp Method

Have you noticed that we seem to be repeating ourself with these unit tests? For each one we are loading a response variable. That seems wasteful and prone to errors. It'd be better to stick to something more DRY (Don't Repeat Yourself).

Since the unit tests are executed top-to-bottom we can add a setUp method that will be run before every test. It will set self.response to our homepage so we no longer need to define a response variable for each test. This also means we can remove the test_homepage_url_name test since we're using the reverse on home each time in setUp.

Code

```python
# pages/tests.py
from django.test import SimpleTestCase
from django.urls import reverse


class HomepageTests(SimpleTestCase): # new

    def setUp(self):
        url = reverse('home')
        self.response = self.client.get(url)

    def test_homepage_status_code(self):
        self.assertEqual(self.response.status_code, 200)

    def test_homepage_template(self):
        self.assertTemplateUsed(self.response, 'home.html')

    def test_homepage_contains_correct_html(self):
        self.assertContains(self.response, 'Homepage')

    def test_homepage_does_not_contain_incorrect_html(self):
        self.assertNotContains(
            self.response, 'Hi there! I should not be on the page.')
```

Now run the tests again. Because setUp is a helper method and does not start with test it will not be considered a unit test in the final tally. So only 4 tests will run.

Command Line

```
$ docker-compose exec web python manage.py test pages
Creating test database for alias 'default'...
System check identified no issues (0 silenced).
....
----------------------------------------------------------------------
Ran 4 tests in 0.278s

OK
Destroying test database for alias 'default'...
```

Resolve

A final views check we can do is that our `HomePageView` "resolves" a given URL path. Django contains the utility function resolve[65] for just this purpose. We will need to import both `resolve` as well as the `HomePageView` at the top of the file.

Our actual test, `test_homepage_url_resolves_homepageview`, checks that the name of the view used to resolve / matches `HomePageView`.

Code
```python
# pages/tests.py
from django.test import SimpleTestCase
from django.urls import reverse, resolve # new
from .views import HomePageView # new


class HomepageTests(SimpleTestCase):

    def setUp(self):
        url = reverse('home')
        self.response = self.client.get(url)

    def test_homepage_status_code(self):
        self.assertEqual(self.response.status_code, 200)

    def test_homepage_template(self):
        self.assertTemplateUsed(self.response, 'home.html')

    def test_homepage_contains_correct_html(self):
        self.assertContains(self.response, 'Homepage')

    def test_homepage_does_not_contain_incorrect_html(self):
        self.assertNotContains(
            self.response, 'Hi there! I should not be on the page.')

    def test_homepage_url_resolves_homepageview(self): # new
        view = resolve('/')
        self.assertEqual(
            view.func.__name__,
            HomePageView.as_view().__name__
        )
```

---

[65]https://docs.djangoproject.com/en/3.1/ref/urlresolvers/#resolve

Phew. That's our last test. Let's confirm that everything passes.

Command Line

```
$ docker-compose exec web python manage.py test
Creating test database for alias 'default'...
System check identified no issues (0 silenced).
.....
------------------------------------------------------------------
Ran 7 tests in 0.282s

OK
Destroying test database for alias 'default'...
```

Git

Time to add our new changes to source control with Git.

Command Line

```
$ git status
$ git add .
$ git commit -m 'ch4'
```

You can compare with the official source code on Github[66] for this chapter.

Conclusion

We have configured our templates and added the first page to our project, a static homepage. We also added tests which should *always* be included with new code changes. Some developers prefer a method called Test-Driven Development where they write the tests first and then the code. Personally I prefer to write the tests *immediately after* which is what we'll do here.

---

[66]https://github.com/wsvincent/djangoforprofessionals/tree/master/ch4-pages

Both approaches work, the key thing is to be rigorous with your testing. Django projects quickly grow in size where it's impossible to remember all the working pieces in your head. And if you are working on a team, it is a nightmare to work on an untested codebase. Who knows what will break?

In the next chapter we'll add user registration to our project: log in, log out, and sign up.

Chapter 5: User Registration

User registration is a core feature in any dynamic website. And it will be in our Bookstore project, too. In this chapter we will implement log in, log out, and sign up functionality. The first two are relatively straightforward since Django provides us with the necessary views and urls for them, however sign up is more challenging since there is no built-in solution.

Auth App

Let's begin by implementing log in and log out using Django's own auth[67] app. Django provides us with the necessary views and urls which means we only need to update a template for things to work. This saves us a lot of time as developers and it ensures that we don't make a mistake since the underlying code has already been tested and used by millions of developers.

However this simplicity comes at the cost of feeling "magical" to Django newcomers. We covered some of these steps previously in my book, Django for Beginners[68], but we did not slow down and look at the underlying source code. The intention for a beginner was to broadly explain and demonstrate "how" to implement user registration properly, but this came at the cost of truly diving into "why" we used the code we did.

Since this is a more advanced book, we delve deeper to understand the underlying source code better. The approach here can also be used to explore any other built-in Django functionality on your own.

The first thing we need to do is make sure the auth app is included in our INSTALLED_APPS setting. We have added our own apps here previously, but have you ever taken a close look at the built-in apps Django adds automatically for us? Most likely the answer is no. Let's do that now!

---

[67]https://docs.djangoproject.com/en/3.1/topics/auth/default/
[68]https://djangoforbeginners.com

Code

```
# config/settings.py
INSTALLED_APPS = [
    'django.contrib.admin',
    'django.contrib.auth', # Yoohoo!!!!
    'django.contrib.contenttypes',
    'django.contrib.sessions',
    'django.contrib.messages',
    'django.contrib.staticfiles',

    # Local
    'accounts',
    'pages',
]
```

There are, in fact, 6 apps already there that Django provides for us which power the site. The first is admin and the second is auth. This is how we know the auth app is already present in our Django project.

When we earlier ran the migrate command for the first time all of these apps were linked together in the initial database. And remember that we used the AUTH_USER_MODEL setting to tell Django to use our custom user model, not the default User model here. This is why we had to wait until that configuration was complete before running migrate for the first time.

Auth URLs and Views

To use Django's built-in auth app we must explicitly add it to our config/urls.py file. The easiest approach is to use accounts/ as the prefix since that is commonly used in the Django community. Make the one line change below. Note that as our urls.py file grows in length, adding comments for each type of URL–admin, user management, local apps, etc.–helps with readability.

Code

```
# config/urls.py
from django.contrib import admin
from django.urls import path, include

urlpatterns = [
    # Django admin
    path('admin/', admin.site.urls),

    # User management
    path('accounts/', include('django.contrib.auth.urls')), # new

    # Local apps
    path('', include('pages.urls')),
]
```

What's included in the `auth` app? A lot it turns out. First off, there are a number of associated urls.

Code

```
accounts/login/ [name='login']
accounts/logout/ [name='logout']
accounts/password_change/ [name='password_change']
accounts/password_change/done/ [name='password_change_done']
accounts/password_reset/ [name='password_reset']
accounts/password_reset/done/ [name='password_reset_done']
accounts/reset/<uidb64>/<token>/ [name='password_reset_confirm']
accounts/reset/done/ [name='password_reset_complete']
```

How did I know that? Two ways. The first is the official auth docs[69] tell us so! But a second, deeper approach is to look at the Django source code which is available on Github[70]. If we navigate or search around we'll find our way to the auth app itself[71]. And within *that* we can find the `urls.py` file at this link[72] which shows the complete source code.

It takes practice to understand the Django source code, but it is well worth the time.

---

[69]https://docs.djangoproject.com/en/3.1/topics/auth/default/#module-django.contrib.auth.views
[70]https://github.com/django/django
[71]https://github.com/django/django/tree/b9cf764be62e77b4777b3a75ec256f6209a57671/django/contrib/auth
[72]https://github.com/django/django/blob/b9cf764be62e77b4777b3a75ec256f6209a57671/django/contrib/auth/urls.py

Homepage

What's next? Let's update our existing homepage so that it will notify us if a user is already logged in or not which currently can only happen via the admin.

Here is the new code for the `templates/home.html` file. It uses the Django templating engine's if/else[73] tags for basic logic.

Code

```
<!-- templates/home.html -->
{% extends '_base.html' %}

{% block title %}Home{% endblock title %}

{% block content %}
  <h1>Homepage</h1>
  {% if user.is_authenticated %}
    Hi {{ user.email }}!
  {% else %}
    <p>You are not logged in</p>
    <a href="{% url 'login' %}">Log In</a>
  {% endif %}
{% endblock content %}
```

If the user is logged in (authenticated), we display a greeting that says "Hi" and includes their email address. These are both variables[74] which we can use with Django's template engine via double opening {{ and closing }} brackets.

The default `User` contains numerous fields including is_authenticated[75] and email[76] which are referenced here.

And the `logout` and `login` are URL names. The url[77] template tag means if we specify the URL name the link will automatically refer to that URL path. For example, in the previous chapter we

---

[73]https://docs.djangoproject.com/en/3.1/ref/templates/builtins/#if
[74]https://docs.djangoproject.com/en/3.1/topics/templates/#variables
[75]https://docs.djangoproject.com/en/3.1/ref/contrib/auth/#django.contrib.auth.models.User.is_authenticated
[76]https://docs.djangoproject.com/en/3.1/ref/contrib/auth/#django.contrib.auth.models.User.email
[77]https://docs.djangoproject.com/en/3.1/ref/templates/builtins/#url

set the name of our homepage URL to `home` so a link to the homepage would take the format of `{% url 'home' %}`. More on this shortly.

If you look at the homepage now at `http://127.0.0.1:8000/` it will likely show the email address of your superuser account since we used it previously to log in.

Homepage with greeting

In the admin over at `http://127.0.0.1:8000/admin/`, if you click on the "Log out" button in the upper right corner we can log out of the admin and by extension the Django project.

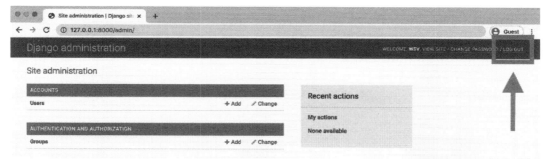

Admin logout link

Return to the homepage at `http://127.0.0.1:8000/` and refresh the page.

Django Source Code

You might have been able to piece together these steps on your own from reading the official docs[78]. But the deeper–and better–approach is to learn how to read the Django source code on your own.

One question is, how was the `user` and its related variables magically available in our template?

---

[78]https://docs.djangoproject.com/en/3.1/topics/auth/default/

The answer is that Django has a concept called the template context[79] which means each template is loaded with data from the corresponding `views.py` file. We can use `user` within template tags to access User attributes. In other words, Django just gives this to us automatically.

So to check if a user is logged in or not, we access `user` and then can use the boolean `is_-authenticated`[80] attribute. If a user is logged in, it will return True and we can do things like display the user's email. Or if no user is logged in, the result will be False.

Moving on we have the URL name `login`. Where did that come from? The answer, of course, is from Django itself! Let's unpack the code snippet `{% url 'login' %}` piece by piece.

First up we're using the url template tag[81] which takes as its first argument a named URL pattern[82]. That's the optional `name` section we add as a best practice to all our URL paths. Therefore there must be a `'login'` name attached to the URL used by Django for log ins, right!

There are two ways we could have known this. In other words, if I hadn't just told you that we wanted to use `{% url 'login' %}`, how could you have figured it out?

First look at the official documentation[83]. Personally I often use the search feature so I would have typed in something like "login" and then clicked around until I found a description of log in. The one we want is actually called authentication views[84] and lists the corresponding URL patterns for us.

---

[79]https://docs.djangoproject.com/en/3.1/topics/auth/default/#authentication-data-in-templates
[80]https://docs.djangoproject.com/en/3.1/ref/contrib/auth/#django.contrib.auth.models.User.is_authenticated
[81]https://docs.djangoproject.com/en/3.1/ref/templates/builtins/#url
[82]https://docs.djangoproject.com/en/3.1/topics/http/urls/#naming-url-patterns
[83]https://docs.djangoproject.com/en/3.1/
[84]https://docs.djangoproject.com/en/3.1/topics/auth/default/#module-django.contrib.auth.views

Code

```
accounts/login/ [name='login']
accounts/logout/ [name='logout']
accounts/password_change/ [name='password_change']
accounts/password_change/done/ [name='password_change_done']
accounts/password_reset/ [name='password_reset']
accounts/password_reset/done/ [name='password_reset_done']
accounts/reset/<uidb64>/<token>/ [name='password_reset_confirm']
accounts/reset/done/ [name='password_reset_complete']
```

This tells us at the path accounts/login/ is where "login" is located and its name is 'login'. A little confusing at first, but here is the info we need.

Going a step deeper to phase two, we can investigate the underlying Django source code to see "logout" in action. If you perform a search over on Github[85] you'll eventually find the auth app itself[86]. Ok, now let's start by investigating the urls.py file. Here is the link[87] to the complete code:

Code

```python
# django/contrib/auth/urls.py
from django.contrib.auth import views
from django.urls import path

urlpatterns = [
    path('login/', views.LoginView.as_view(), name='login'),
    path('logout/', views.LogoutView.as_view(), name='logout'),

    path('password_change/', views.PasswordChangeView.as_view(),
        name='password_change'),
    path('password_change/done/', views.PasswordChangeDoneView.as_view(),
        name='password_change_done'),
    path('password_reset/', views.PasswordResetView.as_view(),
        name='password_reset'),
    path('password_reset/done/', views.PasswordResetDoneView.as_view(),
        name='password_reset_done'),
    path('reset/<uidb64>/<token>/', views.PasswordResetConfirmView.as_view(),
        name='password_reset_confirm'),
```

---

[85] https://github.com/django/django

[86] https://github.com/django/django/tree/b9cf764be62e77b4777b3a75ec256f6209a57671/django/contrib/auth

[87] https://github.com/django/django/blob/b9cf764be62e77b4777b3a75ec256f6209a57671/django/contrib/auth/urls.py

```
    path('reset/done/', views.PasswordResetCompleteView.as_view(),
        name='password_reset_complete'),
]
```

Here is the underlying code Django uses itself for the `auth` app. I hope you can see that the "logout" route is not magic. It's right there in plain sight, it uses the view `LogoutView` and has the URL name `'logout'`. Not magic at all! Just a little challenging to find the first time.

This three-step process is a great way to learn: either remember the Django shortcut, look it up in the docs, or on occasion dive into the source code and truly understand where all this goodness comes from.

Log In

Back on our basic homepage, click on the "Log In" link and... it results in an error!

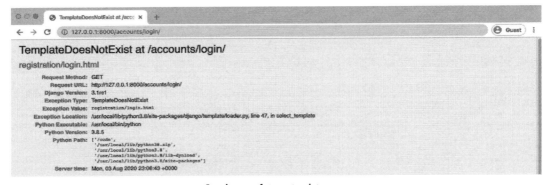

Log in template not exist error

Django is throwing a `TemplateDoesNotExist` error at us. Specifically, it seems to expect a log in template at `registration/login.html`. In addition to Django telling us this, we can look in the documentation[88] and see that the desired `template_name` has that location.

But let's really be sure and check the source code so we can remove any perceived magic here. After all, it's just Django.

---

[88]https://docs.djangoproject.com/en/3.1/topics/auth/default/#all-authentication-views

Back in the auth/views.py[89] file we can see on line 47 for `LoginView` that the `template_name` is `'registration/login.html'`. So if we wanted to change the default location we could, but it would mean overriding `LoginView` which seems like overkill. Let's just use what Django gives us here.

Create a new `registration` folder within the existing `templates` directory and then add our `login.html` file there, too.

Command Line

```
$ mkdir templates/registration
$ touch templates/registration/login.html
```

The actual code is as follows. We extend our base template, add a title, and then specify that we want to use a form that will "post" or send the data.

Code

```html
<!-- templates/registration/login.html -->
{% extends '_base.html' %}

{% block title %}Log In{% endblock title %}

{% block content %}
  <h2>Log In</h2>
  <form method="post">
    {% csrf_token %}
    {{ form.as_p }}
    <button type="submit">Log In</button>
  </form>
{% endblock content %}
```

You should **always** add CSRF protection[90] on any submittable form. Otherwise a malicious website can change the link and attack the site and the user. Django has CSRF middleware to handle this for us; all we need to do is add `{% csrf_token %}` tags at the start of the form.

Next we can control the look of the form contents. For now we'll use as_p()[91] so that each form field is displayed within a paragraph p tag.

---

[89]https://github.com/django/django/blob/b9cf764be62e77b4777b3a75ec256f6209a57671/django/contrib/auth/views.py

[90]https://docs.djangoproject.com/en/3.1/ref/csrf/

[91]https://docs.djangoproject.com/en/3.1/ref/forms/api/#as-p

With that explanation out of the way, let's check if our new template is working correctly. Refresh the web page at `http://127.0.0.1:8000/accounts/login/`.

Log in page

And there is our page! Lovely. You can navigate back to the homepage and confirm that the "Log In" link works, too, if you like. As a final step, go ahead and try to log in with your superuser account on the log in page.

Redirects

Did you notice I said "try" in that last sentence? If you click on the "Log In" link it brings up a `Page not found (404)` error.

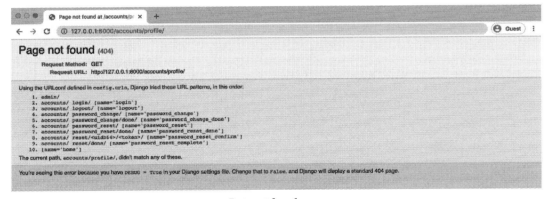

Page not found error

Django has redirected us to `127.0.0.1:8000/accounts/profile/` yet no such page exists. Now why would Django do this? Well, if you think about it, how does Django know where we want to redirect the user after log in? Maybe it's the homepage. But maybe it's a user profile page. Or any number of options.

The final piece of the log in puzzle is to set the proper configuration for LOGIN_REDIRECT_-URL[92] because by default it redirects to `accounts/profile`.

Fortunately, this is a quick fix. We'll send the user to our homepage. And since we specified a URL name of `home` that's all we need to redirect logged in users to the homepage.

At the bottom of the `config/settings.py` file add this one line.

Code

```
# config/settings.py
LOGIN_REDIRECT_URL = 'home'
```

Attempt to log in again at `http://127.0.0.1:8000/accounts/login/`. Upon success it redirects the user to the homepage greeting the superuser account you just logged in with!

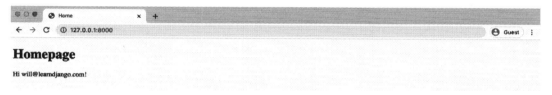

Homepage logged out

Log Out

Now let's add a log out option to our homepage since only a superuser will have access to the admin. How do we do this?

If you look at the `auth` views above we can see that logout uses `LogoutView`, which we could explore in the source code, and has a URL name of `logout`. That means we can refer to it with a template tag as just `logout`.

But we can set this ourself, if desired, using LOGOUT_REDIRECT_URL[93] which can be added to the bottom of our `config/settings.py` file. Let's do that so a logged out user is redirected to the homepage.

---

[92]https://docs.djangoproject.com/en/3.1/ref/settings/#login-redirect-url
[93]https://docs.djangoproject.com/en/3.1/ref/settings/#logout-redirect-url

Code

```
# config/settings.py
LOGIN_REDIRECT_URL = 'home'
LOGOUT_REDIRECT_URL = 'home' # new
```

Then add the logout link to `templates/home.html`.

Code

```
<!-- templates/home.html -->
{% extends '_base.html' %}

{% block title %}Home{% endblock title %}

{% block content %}
  <h1>Homepage</h1>
  {% if user.is_authenticated %}
    Hi {{ user.email }}!
    <p><a href="{% url 'logout' %}">Log Out</a></p>
  {% else %}
    <p>You are not logged in</p>
    <a href="{% url 'login' %}">Log In</a>
  {% endif %}
{% endblock content %}
```

Refresh the homepage at `http://127.0.0.1:8000/` and the "Log out" link is now visible.

Homepage with logout link

If you click on it you will be logged out and redirected to the homepage, which has the "Log In" link visible.

Homepage with login link

Sign Up

Implementing a sign up page for user registration is completely up to us. We'll go through the standard steps for any new page:

- create an app-level `accounts/urls.py` file
- update the project-level `config/urls.py` to point to the `accounts` app
- add a view called `SignupPageView`
- create a `signup.html` template
- update `home.html` to display the sign up page

A common question is: what's the right order for implementing these steps? Honestly it doesn't matter since we need *all* of them for the sign up page to work properly. Generally, I like to start with `urls`, then switch to `views`, and finally `templates` but it's a matter of personal preference.

To start create a `urls.py` file within the `accounts` app. Up to this point it only contains our `CustomUser` in the `models.py` file; we haven't configured any routes or views.

Command Line

```
$ touch accounts/urls.py
```

The URL path for the sign up page will take a view called `SignupPageView` (which we'll create next), at the route `signup/`, and have a `name` of `signup` which we can later use to refer to the page with a `url` template tag. The existing url names for `login` and `signup` are written within the built-in Django app file `django/contrib/auth/urls.py` we saw above.

Code

```
# accounts/urls.py
from django.urls import path
from .views import SignupPageView

urlpatterns = [
    path('signup/', SignupPageView.as_view(), name='signup'),
]
```

Next update the config/urls.py file to include the accounts app. We can create any route we like but it's common to use the same accounts/ one used by the default auth app. Note that it's important to include the path for accounts.urls below: URL paths are loaded top-to-bottom so this ensures that any auth URL paths will be loaded first.

Code

```
# config/urls.py
from django.contrib import admin
from django.urls import path, include

urlpatterns = [
    # Django admin
    path('admin/', admin.site.urls),

    # User management
    path('accounts/', include('django.contrib.auth.urls')),

    # Local apps
    path('accounts/', include('accounts.urls')), # new
    path('', include('pages.urls')),
]
```

Now create the view SignupPageView. It references the CustomUserCreationForm and has a success_url that points to the login page, meaning after the form is submitted the user will be redirected there. The template_name will be signup.html.

Code

```python
# accounts/views.py
from django.urls import reverse_lazy
from django.views import generic
from .forms import CustomUserCreationForm


class SignupPageView(generic.CreateView):
    form_class = CustomUserCreationForm
    success_url = reverse_lazy('login')
    template_name = 'registration/signup.html'
```

As a final step create a file called `signup.html` file within the existing `registration/` directory.

Command Line

```
$ touch templates/registration/signup.html
```

The code is basically identical to the log in page.

Code

```html
<!-- templates/registration/signup.html -->
{% extends '_base.html' %}

{% block title %}Sign Up{% endblock title %}

{% block content %}
  <h2>Sign Up</h2>
  <form method="post">
    {% csrf_token %}
    {{ form.as_p }}
    <button type="submit">Sign Up</button>
  </form>
{% endblock content %}
```

As a final step we can add a line for "Sign Up" to our `home.html` template right below the link for "Log In". This is a one-line change.

Code

```html
<!-- templates/home.html -->
{% extends '_base.html' %}

{% block title %}Home{% endblock title %}

{% block content %}
  <h1>Homepage</h1>
  {% if user.is_authenticated %}
    Hi {{ user.email }}!
    <p><a href="{% url 'logout' %}">Log Out</a></p>
  {% else %}
    <p>You are not logged in</p>
    <a href="{% url 'login' %}">Log In</a>
    <a href="{% url 'signup' %}">Sign Up</a>
  {% endif %}
{% endblock content %}
```

All done! Reload the homepage to see our work.

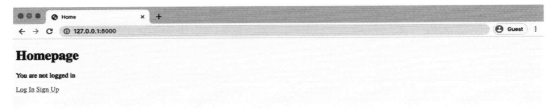

Homepage with Signup

The "Sign Up" link will redirect us to `http://127.0.0.1:8000/accounts/signup/`.

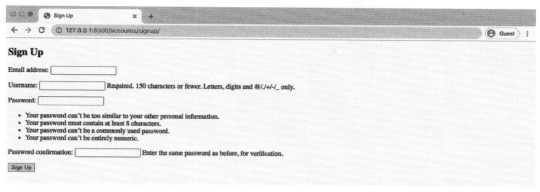

Signup page

Create a new user with the email address `testuser@email.com`, username of `testuser`, and `testpass123` for the password. Upon submission it will redirect us to the Log In page. Log in with the new account and it redirects to the homepage with a personalized greeting.

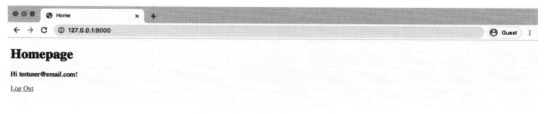

Homepage with testuser greeting

Tests

For tests we do *not* need to test log in and log out features since those are built into Django and already have tests. We *do* need to test our sign up functionality though!

Let's start by creating a `setUp` method that loads our page. Then we'll populate `test_signup_template` with tests for the status code, template used, and both included and excluded text similarly to how we did it in the last chapter for the homepage.

In your text editor, update the `accounts/tests.py` file with these changes.

Code

```python
# accounts/tests.py
from django.contrib.auth import get_user_model
from django.test import TestCase
from django.urls import reverse # new


class CustomUserTests(TestCase):
    ...


class SignupPageTests(TestCase): # new

    def setUp(self):
        url = reverse('signup')
        self.response = self.client.get(url)

    def test_signup_template(self):
        self.assertEqual(self.response.status_code, 200)
        self.assertTemplateUsed(self.response, 'registration/signup.html')
        self.assertContains(self.response, 'Sign Up')
        self.assertNotContains(
            self.response, 'Hi there! I should not be on the page.')
```

Then run our tests.

Command Line

```
$ docker-compose exec web python manage.py test
Creating test database for alias 'default'...
System check identified no issues (0 silenced).
........
----------------------------------------------------------------------
Ran 8 tests in 0.329s

OK
Destroying test database for alias 'default'...
```

Next we can test that our `CustomUserCreationForm` is being used and that the page resolves to `SignupPageView`.

Code

```python
# accounts/tests.py
from django.contrib.auth import get_user_model
from django.test import TestCase
from django.urls import reverse, resolve # new
from .forms import CustomUserCreationForm # new
from .views import SignupPageView # new


class CustomUserTests(TestCase):
    ...


class SignupPageTests(TestCase):

    def setUp(self):
        url = reverse('signup')
        self.response = self.client.get(url)

    def test_signup_template(self):
        self.assertEqual(self.response.status_code, 200)
        self.assertTemplateUsed(self.response, 'signup.html')
        self.assertContains(self.response, 'Sign Up')
        self.assertNotContains(
            self.response, 'Hi there! I should not be on the page.')

    def test_signup_form(self): # new
        form = self.response.context.get('form')
        self.assertIsInstance(form, CustomUserCreationForm)
        self.assertContains(self.response, 'csrfmiddlewaretoken')

    def test_signup_view(self): # new
        view = resolve('/accounts/signup/')
        self.assertEqual(
            view.func.__name__,
            SignupPageView.as_view().__name__
        )
```

Run our tests again.

Command Line

```
$ docker-compose exec web python manage.py test
Creating test database for alias 'default'...
System check identified no issues (0 silenced).
..........
----------------------------------------------------------------------
Ran 10 tests in 0.328s

OK
Destroying test database for alias 'default'...
```

All done.

setUpTestData()

Django 1.8 introduced a major update to TestCase[94] that added the ability to run tests both within a whole class and for each individual test. In particular, setUpTestData()[95] allows the creation of initial data at the class level that can be applied to the entire `TestCase`. This results in much faster tests than using `setUp()`, however, care must be taken not to modify any objects created in `setUpTestData()` in your test methods.

We will use `setUp()` in this book, but be aware that if your test suite seems sluggish a potential optimization to look into is using `setUpTestData()`

Git

As ever make sure to save our work by adding changes into Git.

---

[94]https://docs.djangoproject.com/en/3.1/releases/1.8/#testcase-data-setup

[95]https://docs.djangoproject.com/en/3.1/topics/testing/tools/#django.test.TestCase.setUpTestData

Command Line

```
$ git status
$ git add .
$ git commit -m 'ch5'
```

The official source code is located on Github[96] if you want to compare your code.

Conclusion

Our Bookstore project is not the most beautiful site in the world, but it is very functional at this point. In the next chapter we'll configure our static assets and add Bootstrap for improved styling.

[96]https://github.com/wsvincent/djangoforprofessionals/tree/master/ch5-user-registration

Chapter 6: Static Assets

Static assets like CSS, JavaScript, and images are a core component of any website and Django provides us with a large degree of flexibility around their configuration and storage. In this chapter we'll configure our initial static assets and add Bootstrap[97] to our project for improved styling.

staticfiles app

Django relies on the staticfiles app[98] to manage static files from across our entire project, make them accessible for rapid local development on the file system, and also combine them into a single location that can be served in a better performing manner in production. This process and the distinction between local and production static files confuses many Django newcomers.

To start we'll update the staticfiles app[99] configuration in `settings.py`.

STATIC_URL

The first static file setting, STATIC_URL[100], is already included for us in the `config/settings.py` file.

[97]https://getbootstrap.com/

[98]https://docs.djangoproject.com/en/3.1/ref/contrib/staticfiles/

[99]https://docs.djangoproject.com/en/3.1/ref/settings/#static-files

[100]https://docs.djangoproject.com/en/3.1/ref/settings/#static-url

Code

```
# config/settings.py
STATIC_URL = '/static/'
```

This sets the URL that we can use to reference static files. Note that it is important to include a trailing slash / at the end of the directory name.

STATICFILES_DIRS

Next up is STATICFILES_DIRS[101] which defines the location of static files in *local development*. In our project these will all live within a top-level static directory.

Code

```
# config/settings.py
STATIC_URL = '/static/'
STATICFILES_DIRS = (str(BASE_DIR.joinpath('static')),) # new
```

It's often the case that there will be multiple directories with static files within a project so Python brackets [], which denote a list[102], are typically added here to accommodate future additions.

STATIC_ROOT

STATIC_ROOT[103] is the location of static files for *production* so it must be set to a different name, typically staticfiles. When it comes time to deploy a Django project, the collectstatic[104] command will automatically compile all available static files throughout the entire project into a single directory. This is far faster than having static files sprinkled across the project as is the case in local development.

---

[101]https://docs.djangoproject.com/en/3.1/ref/settings/#staticfiles-dirs
[102]https://docs.python.org/3/tutorial/datastructures.html#more-on-lists
[103]https://docs.djangoproject.com/en/3.1/ref/settings/#static-root
[104]https://docs.djangoproject.com/en/3.1/ref/contrib/staticfiles/#django-admin-collectstatic

Code

```
# config/settings.py
STATIC_URL = '/static/'
STATICFILES_DIRS = (str(BASE_DIR.joinpath('static')),)
STATIC_ROOT = str(BASE_DIR.joinpath('staticfiles')) # new
```

STATICFILES_FINDERS

The last setting is STATICFILES_FINDERS[105], which tells Django how to look for static file directories. It is implicitly set for us and although this is an optional step, I prefer to make it explicit in all projects.

Code

```
# config/settings.py
STATICFILES_FINDERS = [
    "django.contrib.staticfiles.finders.FileSystemFinder",
    "django.contrib.staticfiles.finders.AppDirectoriesFinder",
]
```

The FileSystemFinder looks within the STATICFILES_DIRS setting, which we set to static, for any static files. Then the AppDirectoriesFinder looks for any directories named static located within an app, as opposed to located at a project-level static directory. This setting is read top-to-bottom meaning if a file called static/img.jpg is first found by FileSystemFinder it will be in place of an img.jpg file located within, say, the pages app at pages/static/img.jpg.

Our final group of settings therefore should look as follows:

---

[105]https://docs.djangoproject.com/en/3.1/ref/settings/#staticfiles-finders

Code

```
# config/settings.py
STATIC_URL = '/static/'
STATICFILES_DIRS = (str(BASE_DIR.joinpath('static')),)
STATIC_ROOT = str(BASE_DIR.joinpath('staticfiles')) # new
STATICFILES_FINDERS = [ # new
    "django.contrib.staticfiles.finders.FileSystemFinder",
    "django.contrib.staticfiles.finders.AppDirectoriesFinder",
]
```

Static Directory

Let's now add some static files and incorporate them into our project. Even though we're referring to a static directory for our files it's up to us to create it so do that now along with new subdirectories for CSS, JavaScript, and images.

Command Line

```
$ mkdir static
$ mkdir static/css
$ mkdir static/js
$ mkdir static/images
```

Next create a base.css file.

Command Line

```
$ touch static/css/base.css
```

We'll keep things basic and have our h1 headline be red. The point is to show how CSS can be added to our project, not to delve too deeply into CSS itself.

Code

```
/* static/css/base.css */
h1 {
  color: red;
}
```

If you refresh the homepage now you'll see that nothing has changed. That's because static assets must be explicitly loaded into the templates. First load all static files at the top of the page with {% load static %} and then include a link to the base.css file. The static[106] template tag uses STATIC_URL, which we set to /static/, so rather than needing to write out static/css/base.css we can simply refer to css/base.css.

Code

```
<!-- templates/_base.html -->
{% load static %}
<!DOCTYPE html>
<html>
<head>
  <meta charset="utf-8">
  <title>{% block title %}Bookstore{% endblock %}</title>
  <!-- CSS -->
  <link rel="stylesheet" href="{% static 'css/base.css' %}">
</head>
...
```

Refresh the homepage to see our work. There's our CSS in action!

Homepage with red text

If instead you see an error screen saying Invalid block tag on line 7: 'static'. Did you forget to register or load this tag? then you forgot to include the line {% load static %} at the top of the file. I do this all the time myself.

---

[106]https://docs.djangoproject.com/en/3.1/ref/templates/builtins/#std:templatetag-static

Images

How about an image? You can download the book cover for *Django for Professionals* at this link[107]. Save it into the directory books/static/images as dfp.jpg.

To display it on the homepage, update templates/home.html. Add both the {% load static %} tags at the top and on the next-to-last line the <img> link for the file.

Code

```
<!-- templates/home.html -->
{% extends '_base.html' %}
{% load static %}

{% block title %}Home{% endblock title %}

{% block content %}
  <h1>Homepage</h1>
  <img class="bookcover" src="{% static 'images/dfp.jpg' %}">
  {% if user.is_authenticated %}
    <p>Hi {{ user.email }}!</p>
    <p><a href="{% url 'logout' %}">Log Out</a></p>
  {% else %}
    <p>You are not logged in</p>
    <p><a href="{% url 'login' %}">Log In</a> |
      <a href="{% url 'signup' %}">Sign Up</a></p>
  {% endif %}
{% endblock content %}
```

Refreshing the homepage you'll see the raw file is quite large! Let's control that with some additional CSS.

---

[107]https://learndjango.com/static/images/books/dfp_cover_31.jpg

Code

```
/* static/css/base.css */
h1 {
  color: red;
}

.bookcover {
  height: 300px;
  width: auto;
}
```

Now update the homepage and the book cover image fits nicely.

Homepage with Book Cover

JavaScript

To add JavaScript we'll go through a similar process. Create a new file called base.js.

Command Line

```
$ touch static/js/base.js
```

Often I put a tracking code of some kind here, such as for Google Analytics, but for demonstration purposes we'll add a `console.log` statement so we can confirm the JavaScript loaded correctly.

Code

```javascript
// static/js/base.js
console.log('JavaScript here!')
```

Now add it to our `_base.html` template. JavaScript should be added at the bottom of the file so it is loaded last, after the HTML, CSS, and other assets that appear first on the screen when rendered in the web browser. This gives the appearance of the complete webpage loading faster.

Code

```html
<!-- templates/_base.html -->
{% load static %}
<!DOCTYPE html>
<html>
<head>
  <meta charset="utf-8">
  <title>{% block title %}Bookstore{% endblock title %}</title>
  <!-- CSS -->
  <link rel="stylesheet" href="{% static 'css/base.css' %}">
</head>
<body>
  <div class="container">
    {% block content %}
    {% endblock content %}
  </div>
  <!-- JavaScript -->
  <script src="{% static 'js/base.js' %}"></script>
</body>
</html>
```

In your web browser, make the JavaScript console available. This involves opening up Developer Tools and making sure you're on the "Console" section. On Chrome which is being used for the images in this book, go to View in the top menu, then Developer -> Developer Tools which will open a sidebar. Make sure Console is selected from the options.

If you refresh the page, you should see the following:

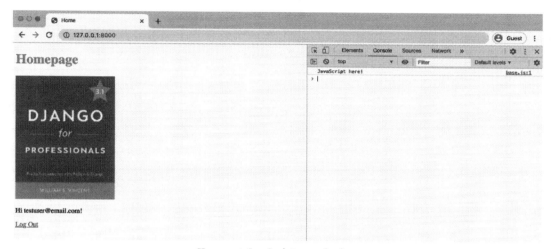

Homepage JavaScript console view

collectstatic

Imagine we wanted to deploy our website right away. Among other steps, we'd need to run collectstatic[108] to create a single, production-ready directory of all the static files in our project.

Command Line

```
$ docker-compose exec web python manage.py collectstatic

135 static files copied to '/code/staticfiles'.
```

If you look within your text editor, there is now a staticfiles directory with four subdirectories: admin, css, images, and js. The first one is the static assets of the Django admin app and the other three we specified. That's why there are 122 files copied over.

---

[108]https://docs.djangoproject.com/en/3.1/ref/contrib/staticfiles/#collectstatic

Bootstrap

Writing custom CSS for your website is a worthy goal and something I advise all software developers, even back-end ones, to try at some point. But practically speaking there is a reason front-end frameworks like Bootstrap[109] exist: they save you a ton of time when starting a new project. Unless you have a dedicated designer to collaborate with, stick with a framework for the early iterations of your website.

In this section we'll add Bootstrap to our project alongside our existing `base.css` file. Typing all this out by hand would take a while and be error prone so this is a rare case where I advise simply copy/pasting from the official source code[110].

Note that order matters here for both the CSS and JavaScript. The file will be loaded top-to-bottom so our `base.css` file comes *after* the Bootstrap CSS so our `h1` style overrides the Bootstrap default. At the bottom of the file, it's similarly important to load jQuery first, then PopperJS, and only then the Bootstrap JavaScript file.

Finally, observe that a navigation header has been added to the project with basic logic so if a user is logged in, only the "Log Out" link is visible while a logged out user will see both "Log In" and "Sign Up" links.

Code

```
<!-- templates/_base.html -->
{% load static %}
<!DOCTYPE html>
<html>
<head>
  <meta charset="utf-8">
  <title>{% block title %}Bookstore{% endblock title %}</title>
  <meta name="viewport" content="width=device-width, initial-scale=1,
  shrink-to-fit=no">
  <!-- CSS -->
  <link rel="stylesheet" href="https://stackpath.bootstrapcdn.com/bootstrap/\
4.5.0/css/bootstrap.min.css" integrity="sha384-9aIt2nRpC12Uk9gS9baDl411\
NQApFmC26EwAOH8WgZl5MYYxFfc+NcPb1dKGj7Sk" crossorigin="anonymous">
```

---

[109]https://getbootstrap.com/

[110]https://github.com/wsvincent/djangoforprofessionals/blob/master/ch6-static-assets/templates/_base.html

```
    <link rel="stylesheet" href="{% static 'css/base.css' %}">
  </head>
  <body>
    <header>
      <!-- Fixed navbar -->
      <div class="d-flex flex-column flex-md-row align-items-center p-3 px-md-4
      mb-3 bg-white border-bottom shadow-sm">
        <a href="{% url 'home' %}" class="navbar-brand my-0 mr-md-auto
        font-weight-normal">Bookstore</a>
        <nav class="my-2 my-md-0 mr-md-3">
          <a class="p-2 text-dark" href="#">About</a>
          {% if user.is_authenticated %}
            <a class="p-2 text-dark" href="{% url 'logout' %}">Log Out</a>
          {% else %}
            <a class="p-2 text-dark" href="{% url 'login' %}">Log In</a>
            <a class="btn btn-outline-primary"
              href="{% url 'signup' %}">Sign Up</a>
          {% endif %}
        </nav>
      </div>
    </header>
    <div class="container">
      {% block content %}
      {% endblock content %}
    </div>
    <!-- JavaScript -->
    <!-- jQuery first, then Popper.js, then Bootstrap JS -->
    <script src="https://code.jquery.com/jquery-3.5.1.slim.min.js"
    integrity="sha384-VCmXjywReHh4PwowAiWNagnWcLhlEJLA5buUprzK8rxF\
    geH0kww/aWY76TfkUoSX" crossorigin="anonymous"></script>
    <script src="https://cdn.jsdelivr.net/npm/popper.js@1.16.1/dist/umd/\
    popper.min.js" integrity="sha384-9/reFTGAW83EW2RDu2S0VKaIzap3H66lZ\
    H81PoYlFhbGU+6BZp6G7niu735Sk7lN" crossorigin="anonymous"></script>
    <script src="https://stackpath.bootstrapcdn.com/bootstrap/4.5.1/js/\
    bootstrap.min.js" integrity="sha384-1CmrxMRARb6aLqgBO7yyAxTOQE2AKb\
    9GfXnEo760AUcUmFx3ibVJJAzGytlQcNXd" crossorigin="anonymous"></script>
  </body>
</html>
```

It's best not to attempt to type this code. Instead copy and paste it from the official repo[111] with one noticeable change: on line 18 of the source code, make sure to change the href tag to #, not

---

[111]https://github.com/wsvincent/djangoforprofessionals/blob/master/ch6-static-assets/templates/_base.html

{% url 'about' %}. In other words, it should match the above code and look like this:

Code

```
<!-- templates/_base.html -->
<a class="p-2 text-dark" href="#">About</a>
```

We'll add the about page URL route in the next section. If you refresh the homepage after making these changes it should look as follows:

Homepage with Bootstrap

About Page

Did you notice the navbar link for an About page? Trouble is the page and the link don't exist yet. But because we already have a handy `pages` app it's quite quick to make one.

Since this will be a static page we don't need a database model involved. However we will need a template, view, and url. Let's start with the template called `about.html`.

Command Line

```
$ touch templates/about.html
```

The page will literally just say "About Page" for now while inheriting from `_base.html`.

Code

```
<!-- templates/about.html -->
{% extends '_base.html' %}

{% block title %}About{% endblock title %}

{% block content %}
  <h1>About Page</h1>
{% endblock content %}
```

The view can rely on Django's built-in `TemplateView` just like our homepage.

Code

```
# pages/views.py
from django.views.generic import TemplateView


class HomePageView(TemplateView):
    template_name = 'home.html'


class AboutPageView(TemplateView): # new
    template_name = 'about.html'
```

The URL path will be pretty similar as well: set it to `about/`, import the appropriate view, and provide a URL name of `about`.

Code

```
# pages/urls.py
from django.urls import path

from .views import HomePageView, AboutPageView # new


urlpatterns = [
    path('about/', AboutPageView.as_view(), name='about'), # new
    path('', HomePageView.as_view(), name='home'),
]
```

If now go to `http://127.0.0.1:8000/about/` you can see the About page.

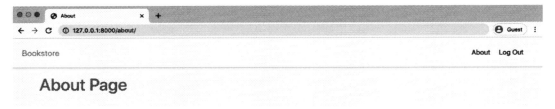

As a final step, update the link in the navbar to the page. Because we provided a name in the URL path of about that's what we'll use.

On line 18 of `_base.html` change the line with the About page link to the following:

Code

```
<!-- templates/_base.html -->
<a class="p-2 text-dark" href="{% url 'about' %}">About</a>
```


Django Crispy Forms

One last update concerns our forms. The popular 3rd party package django-crispy-forms[112] provides a host of welcome upgrades.

[112]https://github.com/django-crispy-forms/django-crispy-forms

We'll follow the usual pattern to install it which is: install within Docker, stop our Docker container and then rebuild it.

Command Line

```
$ docker-compose exec web pipenv install django-crispy-forms==1.9.2
$ docker-compose down
$ docker-compose up -d --build
```

Now add crispy forms to the INSTALLED_APPS setting. Note that it's name needs to be crispy_-forms here. A nice additional feature is to specify bootstrap4 under CRISPY_TEMPLATE_PACK which will provide pre-styled forms for us.

Code

```
# config/settings.py
INSTALLED_APPS = [
    'django.contrib.admin',
    'django.contrib.auth',
    'django.contrib.contenttypes',
    'django.contrib.sessions',
    'django.contrib.messages',
    'django.contrib.staticfiles',

    # Third-party
    'crispy_forms', # new

    # Local
    'accounts',
    'pages',
]

# django-crispy-forms
CRISPY_TEMPLATE_PACK = 'bootstrap4' # new
```

To use Crispy Forms we load crispy_forms_tags at the top of a template and add {{ form|crispy }} to replace {{ form.as_p}} for displaying form fields. We will take this time to also add Bootstrap styling to the Submit button.

Start with signup.html. Make the updates below.

Code

```
<!-- templates/registration/signup.html -->
{% extends '_base.html' %}
{% load crispy_forms_tags %}

{% block title %}Sign Up{% endblock title %}

{% block content %}
  <h2>Sign Up</h2>
  <form method="post">
    {% csrf_token %}
    {{ form|crispy }}
    <button class="btn btn-success" type="submit">Sign Up</button>
  </form>
{% endblock content %}
```

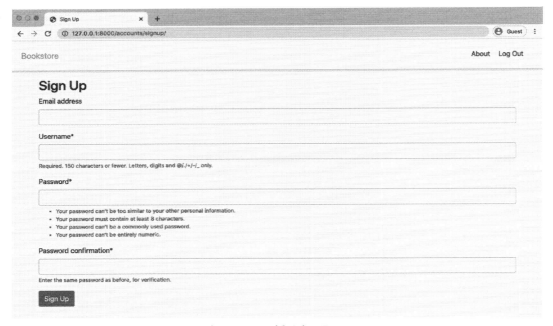

Sign Up Page with Crispy Forms

Update login.html as well with crispy_forms_tags at the top and {{ form|crispy }} in the form.

Code

```
<!-- templates/registration/login.html -->
{% extends '_base.html' %}
{% load crispy_forms_tags %}

{% block title %}Log In{% endblock title %}

{% block content %}
  <h2>Log In</h2>
  <form method="post">
    {% csrf_token %}
    {{ form|crispy }}
    <button class="btn btn-success" type="submit">Log In</button>
  </form>
{% endblock content %}
```

Log In Page with Crispy Forms

Tests

Time for tests which will be very similar to those we added previously for our homepage.

Code

```
# pages/tests.py
from django.test import SimpleTestCase
from django.urls import reverse, resolve
from .views import HomePageView, AboutPageView # new


class HomepageTests(SimpleTestCase):
    ...


class AboutPageTests(SimpleTestCase): # new

    def setUp(self):
        url = reverse('about')
        self.response = self.client.get(url)

    def test_aboutpage_status_code(self):
        self.assertEqual(self.response.status_code, 200)

    def test_aboutpage_template(self):
        self.assertTemplateUsed(self.response, 'about.html')

    def test_aboutpage_contains_correct_html(self):
        self.assertContains(self.response, 'About Page')

    def test_aboutpage_does_not_contain_incorrect_html(self):
        self.assertNotContains(
            self.response, 'Hi there! I should not be on the page.')

    def test_aboutpage_url_resolves_aboutpageview(self):
        view = resolve('/about/')
        self.assertEqual(
            view.func.__name__,
            AboutPageView.as_view().__name__
        )
```

Run the tests.

Command Line

```
$ docker-compose exec web python manage.py test
Creating test database for alias 'default'...
System check identified no issues (0 silenced).
...............
----------------------------------------------------------------
Ran 15 tests in 0.433s

OK
Destroying test database for alias 'default'...
```

Git

Check the status of our changes in this chapter, add them all, and then provide a commit message.

Command Line

```
$ git status
$ git add .
$ git commit -m 'ch6'
```

As alway you can compare your code with the official code on Github[113] if there are any issues.

Conclusion

Static assets are a core part of every website and in Django we have to take a number of additional steps so they are compiled and hosted efficiently in production. Later on in the book we'll learn how to use a dedicated content delivery network (CDN) for hosting and displaying our project's static files.

---

[113]https://github.com/wsvincent/djangoforprofessionals/tree/master/ch6-static-assets

Chapter 7: Advanced User Registration

At this point we have the standard Django user registration implemented. But often that's just the starting point on professional projects. What about customizing things a bit? For example, Django's default username/email/password pattern is somewhat dated these days. It's far more common to simply require email/password for sign up and log in. And really every part of the authentication flow–the forms, emails, pages–can be customized if so desired.

Another major factor in many projects is the need for social authentication, that is handling sign up and log in via a third-party service like Google, Facebook, and so on.

We could implement our own solutions here from scratch but there are some definite risks: user registration is a complex area with many moving parts and one area where we really do not want to make a security mistake.

For this reason, many professional Django developers rely on the popular third-party django-allauth[114]. Adding any third party package should come with a degree of caution since you *are* adding another dependency to your technical stack. It's important to make sure any package is both up-to-date and well tested. Fortunately `django-allauth` is both.

At the cost of a little bit of *magic* it addresses all of these concerns and makes customization much, much easier.

django-allauth

Start by installing `django-allauth`. Because we're using `Pipenv` we want to avoid conflicts with the `Pipfile.lock` so we'll install it within Docker first, then stop Docker, and rebuild our image with the `--build` flag which prevents the default image caching and ensures that our entire image is built from scratch.

---

[114]https://github.com/pennersr/django-allauth

Command Line

```
$ docker-compose exec web pipenv install django-allauth==0.42.0
$ docker-compose down
$ docker-compose up -d --build
```

Our website will still function the same as before since we haven't explicitly told Django about this new `django-allauth` package. To do that we need to update the `INSTALLED_APPS` config within our `settings.py` file adding Django's built-in, but optional, sites framework[115], as well as `allauth` and its account feature `allauth.account`.

Django's sites framework is a powerful feature that allows one Django project to control multiple sites. Given we only have one site in our project, we'll set the `SITE_ID` to 1. If we added a second site it would have an ID of 2, a third site would have an ID of 3, and so on.

Code

```
# config/settings.py
INSTALLED_APPS = [
    'django.contrib.admin',
    'django.contrib.auth',
    'django.contrib.contenttypes',
    'django.contrib.sessions',
    'django.contrib.messages',
    'django.contrib.staticfiles',
    'django.contrib.sites', # new

    # Third-party
    'crispy_forms',
    'allauth', # new
    'allauth.account', # new

    # Local
    'accounts',
    'pages',
]

# django-allauth config
SITE_ID = 1 # new
```

---

[115]https://docs.djangoproject.com/en/3.1/ref/contrib/sites/

AUTHENTICATION_BACKENDS

The `settings.py` file created by Django for any new project contains a number of explicit settings–those that we see in the file already–as well as a longer additional list of implicit settings that exist but aren't visible. This can be confusing at first. The complete list of settings configurations is available here[116].

An example is the AUTHENTICATION_BACKENDS[117] setting. Under the hood Django sets this to `'django.contrib.auth.backends.ModelBackend'`, which is used when Django attempts to authenticate a user. We could add the following line to `settings.py` and the current behavior would remain unchanged:

Code

```
AUTHENTICATION_BACKENDS = (
    'django.contrib.auth.backends.ModelBackend',
)
```

However, for `django-allauth` we need to add its specific authentication options, too, which will allow us to switch over to using login via e-mail in a moment. So at the bottom of your `settings.py` file add the following section:

Code

```
# config/settings.py
# django-allauth config
SITE_ID = 1
AUTHENTICATION_BACKENDS = (
    'django.contrib.auth.backends.ModelBackend',
    'allauth.account.auth_backends.AuthenticationBackend', # new
)
```

---

[116]https://docs.djangoproject.com/en/3.1/ref/settings/

[117]https://docs.djangoproject.com/en/3.1/ref/settings/#authentication-backends

EMAIL_BACKEND

Another configuration implicitly set is EMAIL_BACKEND[118]. By default Django will look for a configured SMTP server[119] to send emails.

django-allauth will send such an email upon a successful user registration, which we can and will customize later, but since we don't *yet* have a SMTP server properly configured, it will result in an error.

The solution, for now, is to have Django output any emails to the command line console instead. Thus we can override the default, implicit config by using console[120] instead of smtp. Add this at the bottom of the settings.py file.

Code

```
# config/settings.py
# django-allauth config
SITE_ID = 1
AUTHENTICATION_BACKENDS = (
    'django.contrib.auth.backends.ModelBackend',
    'allauth.account.auth_backends.AuthenticationBackend',
)
EMAIL_BACKEND = 'django.core.mail.backends.console.EmailBackend' # new
```

ACCOUNT_LOGOUT_REDIRECT

There's one more subtle change to make to our configurations at this time. If you look at the configurations page[121] again you'll see there is a setting for ACCOUNT_LOGOUT_REDIRECT that defaults to the path of the homepage at /.

In our current settings.py file we have the following two lines for redirects which point to the homepage via its URL name of 'home'.

---

[118]https://docs.djangoproject.com/en/3.1/ref/settings/#email-backend
[119]https://en.wikipedia.org/wiki/Simple_Mail_Transfer_Protocol
[120]https://docs.djangoproject.com/en/3.1/topics/email/#console-backend
[121]https://django-allauth.readthedocs.io/en/latest/configuration.html

Code

```
# config/settings.py
LOGIN_REDIRECT_URL = 'home'
LOGOUT_REDIRECT_URL = 'home'
```

The issue is that django-allauth's ACCOUNT_LOGOUT_REDIRECT actually overrides the built-in LOGOUT_REDIRECT_URL, however, since they both point to the homepage this change may not be apparent. To future-proof our application since maybe we don't want to always redirect to the homepage on logout, we should be explicit here with the logout redirect.

We can also move the two redirect lines under our django-allauth config section. This is what the entire django-allauth config section should look like at this time.

Code

```
# config/settings.py
# django-allauth config
LOGIN_REDIRECT_URL = 'home'
ACCOUNT_LOGOUT_REDIRECT = 'home' # new
SITE_ID = 1
AUTHENTICATION_BACKENDS = (
    'django.contrib.auth.backends.ModelBackend',
    'allauth.account.auth_backends.AuthenticationBackend',
)
EMAIL_BACKEND = 'django.core.mail.backends.console.EmailBackend'
```

Given that we have made many changes to our config/settings.py file let's now run migrate to update our database.

Command Line

```
$ docker-compose exec web python manage.py migrate
```

URLs

We also need to swap out the built-in auth app URLs for django-allauth's own allauth app. We'll still use the same accounts/ URL path, however, since we'll be using django allauth's templates and routes for sign up we can delete the URL path for our accounts app, too.

Code

```
# config/urls.py
from django.contrib import admin
from django.urls import path, include

urlpatterns = [
    # Django admin
    path('admin/', admin.site.urls),

    # User management
    path('accounts/', include('allauth.urls')), # new

    # Local apps
    path('', include('pages.urls')),
]
```

At this point we *could* further delete accounts/urls.py and accounts/views.py which were both created solely for our hand-written sign up page and are no longer being used.

Templates

Django's auth app looks for templates within a templates/registration directory, but allauth prefers they be located within a templates/account directory. So we will create a new directory called templates/account and then copy over our existing login.html and signup.html templates into it.

Command Line

```
$ mkdir templates/account
$ mv templates/registration/login.html templates/account/login.html
$ mv templates/registration/signup.html templates/account/signup.html
```

> It's easy to add an s onto account here by accident, but don't or you'll get an error. The correct directory is templates/account/.

We can delete the templates/registration directory at this point since it is no longer needed.

```
$ rm -r templates/registration
```

`rm` means remove and `-r` means do it recursively, which is necessary whenever you are dealing with a directory. If you'd like further information on this command you can type `man rm` to read the manual.

The last step is to update the URL links within `templates/_base.html` and `templates/home.html` to use `django-allauth`'s URL names rather than Django's. We do this by adding an `account_` prefix so Django's `'logout'` will now be `'account_logout'`, `'login'` will be `'account_login'`, and `signup` will be `account_signup`.

Code

```html
<!-- templates/_base.html -->
...
<nav class="my-2 my-md-0 mr-md-3">
  <a class="p-2 text-dark" href="{% url 'about' %}">About</a>
  {% if user.is_authenticated %}
    <a class="p-2 text-dark" href="{% url 'account_logout' %}">Log Out</a>
  {% else %}
    <a class="p-2 text-dark" href="{% url 'account_login' %}">Log In</a>
    <a class="btn btn-outline-primary"
      href="{% url 'account_signup' %}">Sign Up</a>
  {% endif %}
</nav>
...
```

Code

```html
<!-- templates/home.html -->
{% extends '_base.html' %}
{% load static %}

{% block title %}Home{% endblock title %}

{% block content %}
  <h1>Homepage</h1>
  <img class="bookcover" src="{% static 'images/dfp.jpg' %}">
  {% if user.is_authenticated %}
    <p>Hi {{ user.email }}!</p>
    <p><a href="{% url 'account_logout' %}">Log Out</a></p>
  {% else %}
    <p>You are not logged in</p>
    <p><a href="{% url 'account_login' %}">Log In</a> |
    <a href="{% url 'account_signup' %}">Sign Up</a></p>
  {% endif %}
{% endblock content %}
```

And we're done!

Log In

Refresh the homepage at `http://127.0.0.1:8000`, log out if you are already logged in, and click on the "Log in" link. The Log In page is now updated page.

Log In Page

Note the new "Remember Me" box option. This is the first of many configurations[122] that django-allauth provides. The default `None` asks the user if they want their session to be remembered so they don't have to log in again. It can also be set to `False` to not remember or `True` to always remember. We'll choose `True` which is how a traditional Django log in page would work.

Under the `# django-allauth config` section of the `config/settings.py` file add a new line for this.

Code

```
# config/settings.py
# django-allauth config
...
ACCOUNT_SESSION_REMEMBER = True # new
```

Refresh the "Log In" page and the box is gone!

---

[122]https://django-allauth.readthedocs.io/en/latest/configuration.html

Log In Page No Box

If you try out the log in form with your superuser account it will redirect back to the homepage with a welcome message. Click on the "Log Out" link.

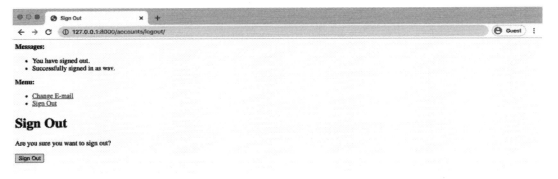

Log Out Page

Rather than directly log us out, `django-allauth` has an intermediary "Log Out" page which we can customize to match the rest of our project.

Log Out

Update the default Log Out template by creating a `templates/account/logout.html` file to override it.

Command Line

```
$ touch templates/account/logout.html
```

Like our other templates it will extend _base.html and include Bootstrap styling on the submitted button.

Code

```
<!-- templates/account/logout.html -->
{% extends '_base.html' %}
{% load crispy_forms_tags %}

{% block title %}Log Out{% endblock %}

{% block content %}
  <h1>Log Out</h1>
  <p>Are you sure you want to log out?</p>
  <form method="post" action="{% url 'account_logout' %}">
    {% csrf_token %}
    {{ form|crispy }}
    <button class="btn btn-danger" type="submit">Log Out</button>
  </form>
{% endblock content %}
```

Go ahead and refresh the page.

Custom Log Out Page

Then click on the "Log Out" link to complete the process.

Sign Up

At the top of our website, in the nav bar, click on link for "Sign Up" which has Bootstrap and `django-crispy-forms` styling.

Sign Up Page

An optional customization we can make via `django-allauth` is to only ask for a password once. Since we'll configure password change and reset options later, there's less of a risk that a user who types in the password incorrectly will be locked out of their account.

This change is, if you look at the django-allauth configuration options[123], is a one-liner.

---

[123]https://django-allauth.readthedocs.io/en/latest/configuration.html

Code

```
# config/settings.py
# django-allauth config
...
ACCOUNT_SIGNUP_PASSWORD_ENTER_TWICE = False # new
```

Refresh the page and the form will update itself to remove the additional password line.

Sign Up with Single Password

Now create a new user to confirm everything works. We can call the user testuser1, use testuser1@email.com as email, and testpass123 as the password.

Upon submit it will redirect you to the homepage.

testuser Homepage

Remember how we configured email to output to the console? `django-allauth` automatically sends an email upon registration which we can view by typing `docker-compose logs`.

Command Line

```
$ docker-compose logs
...
web_1  | Content-Type: text/plain; charset="utf-8"
web_1  | MIME-Version: 1.0
web_1  | Content-Transfer-Encoding: 7bit
web_1  | Subject: [example.com] Please Confirm Your E-mail Address
web_1  | From: webmaster@localhost
web_1  | To: testuser@email.com
web_1  | Date: Mon, 03 Aug 2020 14:04:15 -0000
web_1  | Message-ID: <155266195771.15.17095643701553564393@cdab877c4af3>
web_1  |
web_1  | Hello from example.com!
web_1  |
web_1  | You're receiving this e-mail because user testuser1 has given yours as
an e-mail address to connect their account.
web_1  |
web_1  | To confirm this is correct, go to http://127.0.0.1:8000/accounts/
confirm-emailMQ:1h4oIn:GYETeK5dRClGjcgA8NbuOoyvafA/
web_1  |
web_1  | Thank you from example.com!
web_1  | example.com
```

```
web_1    |   ----------------------------------------------------------------
...
```

There it is. Later on we'll customize this message and configure a proper email service to send it to actual users.

Admin

Log in to the admin with your superuser account at `http://127.0.0.1:8000/admin/` and we can see it, too, has changed now that `django-allauth` is involved.

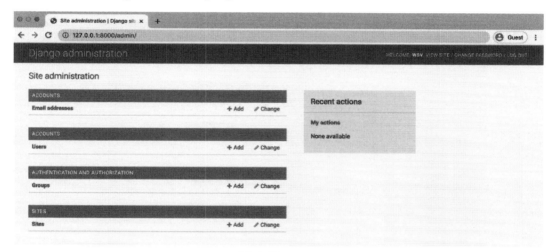

Admin Homepage

There are two new sections: `Accounts` and `Sites` courtesy of our recent work. If you click on the `Users` section we see our traditional view that shows the three current user accounts.

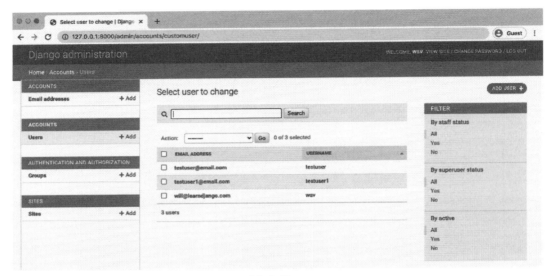

Admin Users

New as of Django 3.1 is the sidebar on the left which means we can go directly to the section for Sites to see what the Django sites framework provides. We'll update both the Domain Name and the Display Name in a later chapter on configuring email.

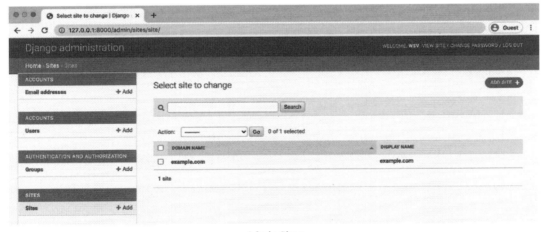

Admin Sites

Email Only Login

It's time to really use django-allauth's extensive list of configurations[124] by switching over to using just email for login, not username. This requires a few changes. First we'll make a username not required, but set email instead to required. Then we'll require email to be unique and the authentication method of choice.

Code

```
# config/settings.py
# django-allauth config
...
ACCOUNT_USERNAME_REQUIRED = False # new
ACCOUNT_AUTHENTICATION_METHOD = 'email' # new
ACCOUNT_EMAIL_REQUIRED = True # new
ACCOUNT_UNIQUE_EMAIL = True # new
```

Navigate back to the homepage and click on "Log Out" since you'll be logged in with your superuser account. Then click on the navbar link for "Sign Up" and create an account for testuser2@email.com with testpass123 as the password.

After being redirected to the homepage upon success, go into the admin to inspect what actually happened. Log in with your superuser account and navigate to the Users section.

---

[124]https://django-allauth.readthedocs.io/en/latest/configuration.html

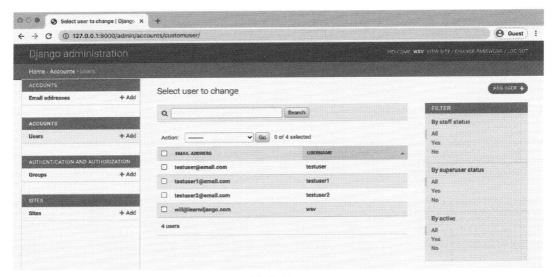

Admin Users

We can see that `django-allauth` automatically populated a username for us based on the email part before the @. This is because our underlying `CustomUser` model still has a `username` field. We didn't delete it.

While this approach may seem a little hackish in fact it works *just fine*. Fully removing the username from the custom user model requires the use of AbstractBaseUser[125], which is an additional, optional step some developers take. It requires far more coding and understanding so it is not recommended unless you really know your way around Django's authentication system!

There is, however, an edge case here that we should confirm which is: what happens if we have `testuser2@email.com` and then a sign up for `testuser2@example.com`? Wouldn't that result in a username of `testuser2` for both which would cause a conflict? Let's try it out!

Log out of the admin, on the Sign Up Page create an account for `testuser2@example.com`.

---

[125]https://docs.djangoproject.com/en/3.1/topics/auth/customizing/#django.contrib.auth.models. AbstractBaseUser

Sign Up Form

Now log back into the admin and go to our `Users` section.

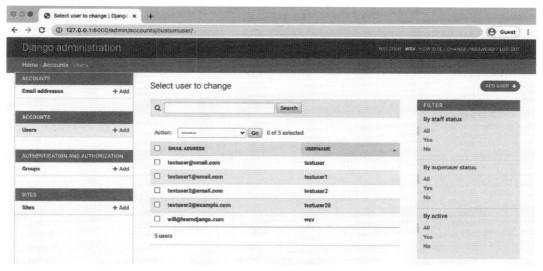

Admin Users

`django-allauth` automtically adds a two-digit string to the username. In this case it is `28` so `testuser2` becomes `testuser28`. This two-digit string will be randomly generated for us.

Tests

Time for tests. Like any good third-party package `django-allauth` comes with its own tests so we don't need to re-test its core functionality, just confirm that our project works as expected.

If you run our current test suite there are 3 errors related to `SignupPageTests` since we're using `django-allauth` now for this rather than our own views, forms, and urls.

Command Line

```
$ docker-compose exec web python manage.py test
...
Ran 15 tests in 0.363s

FAILED (errors=3)
```

Let's update the tests. The first issue is that `signup` is no longer the correct URL name, instead we're using `account_signup` which is the name `django-allauth` provides. How did I know that? I looked at the source code[126] and found the URL name.

The `signup.html` template is also now located at `account/signup.html`. And we're not using `CustomUserCreationForm` anymore, so we can remove that test. Remove as well the imports for `CustomUserCreationForm` and `SignupPageView` at the top of the file.

Code

```
# accounts/tests.py
from django.contrib.auth import get_user_model
from django.test import TestCase
from django.urls import reverse, resolve


class CustomUserTests(TestCase):
    ...


class SignupTests(TestCase): # new

    username = 'newuser'
    email = 'newuser@email.com'
```

---

[126]https://github.com/pennersr/django-allauth/blob/master/allauth/account/urls.py

```python
def setUp(self):
    url = reverse('account_signup')
    self.response = self.client.get(url)

def test_signup_template(self):
    self.assertEqual(self.response.status_code, 200)
    self.assertTemplateUsed(self.response, 'account/signup.html')
    self.assertContains(self.response, 'Sign Up')
    self.assertNotContains(
        self.response, 'Hi there! I should not be on the page.')

def test_signup_form(self):
    new_user = get_user_model().objects.create_user(
        self.username, self.email)
    self.assertEqual(get_user_model().objects.all().count(), 1)
    self.assertEqual(get_user_model().objects.all()
                     [0].username, self.username)
    self.assertEqual(get_user_model().objects.all()
                     [0].email, self.email)
```

Run the tests again.

Command Line

```
$ docker-compose exec web python manage.py test
Creating test database for alias 'default'...
System check identified no issues (0 silenced).
..............
----------------------------------------------------------------
Ran 14 tests in 0.410s

OK
Destroying test database for alias 'default'...
```

Social

If you want to add social authentication it's just a few settings. I have a complete tutorial online[127] for integrating Github. The process is similar for Google, Facebook, and all the rest

---

[127]https://learndjango.com/tutorials/django-allauth-tutorial

`django-allauth` supports. Here is the complete list of providers[128].

Git

As always commit the code changes with Git.

Command Line

```
$ git status
$ git add .
$ git commit -m 'ch7'
```

And if there are any issues, compare with the official source code on Github[129].

Conclusion

We now have a user registration flow that works and can be quickly extended into social authentication if needed. In the next chapter we'll add environment variables to our project for greater security and flexibility.

---

[128]https://django-allauth.readthedocs.io/en/latest/providers.html

[129]https://github.com/wsvincent/djangoforprofessionals/tree/master/ch7-advanced-user-registration

Chapter 8: Environment Variables

Environment variables[130] are variables that can be loaded into the operating environment of a project at run time as opposed to hard coded into the codebase itself. They are considered an integral part of the popular Twelve-Factor App Design[131] methodology and a Django best practice because they allow a greater level of security and simpler local/production configurations.

Why greater security? Because we can store truly secret information–database credentials, API keys, and so on–separate from the actual code base. This is a good idea because using a version control system, like `git`, means that it only takes one bad commit for credentials to be added in there forever. Which means that *anyone* with access to the codebase has full control over the project. This is very, very dangerous. It's much better to limit who has access to the application and environment variables provide an elegant way to do so.

A secondary advantage is that environment variables make it much easier to switch between local and production code environments. As we will see, there are a number of setting configurations that Django uses by default intended to make local development easier, but which must be changed once the same project is ready for production.

]

environs[django]

There are many different ways to work with environment variables in Python but for this project we'll use the environs[132] package, which has a Django-specific option that installs a number of additional packages that help with configuration.

On the command line, install `environs[django]`. Note that you'll probably need to add single quotes `''` around the package if you're using Zsh as your terminal shell, so run `pipenv install`

---

[130]https://en.wikipedia.org/wiki/Environment_variable
[131]https://12factor.net/
[132]https://github.com/sloria/environs

'environs[django]==8.0.0'. We'll also need to spin down our Docker container and rebuild it with the new package.

Command Line

```
$ docker-compose exec web pipenv install 'environs[django]==8.0.0'
$ docker-compose down
$ docker-compose up -d --build
```

In the config/settings.py file, there are three lines of imports to add at the top of the file, just under the import of Path.

Code

```
# config/settings.py
from pathlib import Path
from environs import Env # new

env = Env() # new
env.read_env() # new
```

All set.

SECRET_KEY

For our first environment variable we'll set the SECRET_KEY[133], a randomly generated string used for cryptographic signing[134] and created whenever the startproject command is run. It is very important that SECRET_KEY actually be kept, well, secret.

In my config/settings.py file, it has the following value:

---

[133]https://docs.djangoproject.com/en/3.1/ref/settings/#std:setting-SECRET_KEY
[134]https://docs.djangoproject.com/en/3.1/topics/signing/

Code

```
# config/settings.py
SECRET_KEY = ')*_s#exg*#w+#-xt=vu8b010%%a&p@4edwyj0=(nqq90b9a8*n'
```

Note that the single quotes (") around the SECRET_KEY which make it a Python string. These are not actually part of the SECRET_KEY value itself, which is an easy mistake to make.

There is a two-step process to switching over to environment variables:

- add the environment variable to the docker-compose.yml file
- update config/settings.py to point to the variable

In the docker-compose.yml file, add a section called environment under the web service. It will be a variable that we'll call DJANGO_SECRET_KEY with the value of our existing SECRET_KEY. This is what the updated file looks like:

docker-compose.yml

```
# config/settings.py
version: '3.8'

services:
  web:
    build: .
    command: python /code/manage.py runserver 0.0.0.0:8000
    volumes:
      - .:/code
    ports:
      - 8000:8000
    depends_on:
      - db
    environment:
      - "DJANGO_SECRET_KEY=)*_s#exg*#w+#-xt=vu8b010%%a&p@4edwyj0=(nqq90b9a8*n"
  db:
    image: postgres:11
    volumes:
      - postgres_data:/var/lib/postgresql/data/
    environment:
      - "POSTGRES_HOST_AUTH_METHOD=trust"

volumes:
  postgres_data:
```

> Note that if your SECRET_KEY includes a dollar sign, $, then you need to add an additional dollar sign, $$. This is due to how `docker-compose` handles variable substitution[a]. Otherwise you will see an error!
>
> ---
> [a]https://docs.docker.com/compose/compose-file/#variable-substitution

The second step is to update the SECRET_KEY configuration within `config/settings.py`.

Code

```
# config/settings.py
SECRET_KEY = env("DJANGO_SECRET_KEY")
```

If you refresh the website you'll see everything works as before, which is what we want. If for some reason the SECRET_KEY was not loaded in properly, we'd see an error message as Django requires one to work properly.

Astute readers may notice that even though we are now using an environment variable the actual value of SECRET_KEY is still visible in our source code as it's merely moved to `docker-compose.yml`. This is true! However, when we configure our website for production, we will create a separate file for production purposes–`docker-compose-production.yml`–and load in production environment variables via a `.env` file that is not tracked by Git.

For now though, the goal of this chapter is to start using environment variables locally for the values that need to be either truly secret or switched in a production context.

DEBUG and ALLOWED_HOSTS

As the Django deployment checklist[135] notes, there are a number of settings that must be updated before a website can be deployed safely in production. Chief among them are DEBUG[136] and ALLOWED_HOSTS[137].

---
[135]https://docs.djangoproject.com/en/3.1/howto/deployment/checklist/
[136]https://docs.djangoproject.com/en/3.1/ref/settings/#std:setting-DEBUG
[137]https://docs.djangoproject.com/en/3.1/ref/settings/#allowed-hosts

When DEBUG is set to True, Django displays a lengthy message and detailed bug report whenever an error occurs. For example, try visiting a page that does not exist such as /debug.

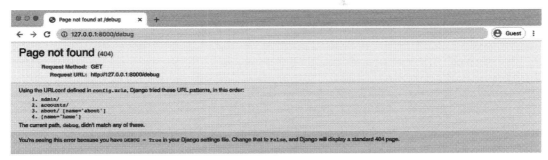

Debug Page

This is great for our purposes as developers, but it is also a roadmap for a hacker in a production setting. When DEBUG is set to False it is required to add a setting for ALLOWED_HOSTS, which controls the specific hosts or domains that can access the website. We'll add the two local ports—localhost and 127.0.0.1—as well as .herokuapp.com, which will be used by Heroku for our production website.

Update the config/settings.py file with two new settings:

Code

```
# config/settings.py
DEBUG = False # new
ALLOWED_HOSTS = ['.herokuapp.com', 'localhost', '127.0.0.1'] # new
```

Then refresh the web page.

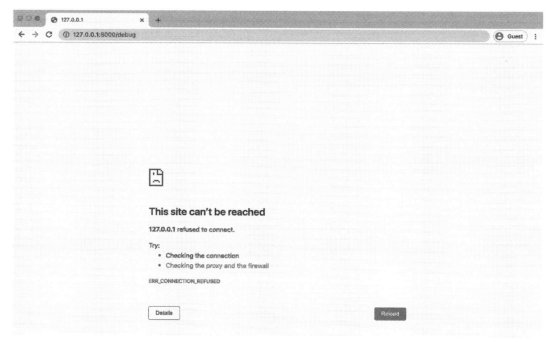

Debug Page Not Found

This is the behavior we want for our live site: no information, just a generic message. When we deploy the website we'll use an elegant way to toggle between the two settings, but for now change DEBUG to an environment variable called DJANGO_DEBUG.

Code

```
# config/settings.py
DEBUG = env.bool("DJANGO_DEBUG")
```

Then proceed to update docker-compose.yml so DJANGO_DEBUG is set to True.

docker-compose.yml

```
version: '3.8'

services:
  web:
    build: .
    command: python /code/manage.py runserver 0.0.0.0:8000
    volumes:
      - .:/code
    ports:
      - 8000:8000
    depends_on:
      - db
    environment:
      - "DJANGO_SECRET_KEY=)*_s#exg*#w+#-xt=vu8b010%%a&p@4edwyj0=(nqq90b9a8*n"
      - "DJANGO_DEBUG=True"
  db:
    image: postgres:11
    volumes:
      - postgres_data:/var/lib/postgresql/data/
    environment:
      - "POSTGRES_HOST_AUTH_METHOD=trust"

volumes:
  postgres_data:
```

After the changes refresh your website and it will work as before.

DATABASES

When we installed environs[django] earlier, the Django "goodies" included the elegant dj-database-url[138] package, which takes all the database configurations needed for our database, SQLite or PostgreSQL. This will be very helpful later on in production.

For now, we can set it to use PostgreSQL locally by adding a default value. Update the existing DATABASES configuration with the following:

---

[138]https://github.com/jacobian/dj-database-url

Code

```
# config/settings.py
DATABASES = {
    "default": env.dj_db_url("DATABASE_URL",
    default="postgres://postgres@db/postgres")
}
```

The environment variable `DATABASE_URL` will be created by Heroku when we deploy. More on that
later.

Refresh the website to confirm everything still works properly.

Git

We made a number of important changes in this chapter so make sure to commit the code
updates with Git.

Command Line

```
$ git status
$ git add .
$ git commit -m 'ch8'
```

If any issues crop up, compare your files against the official source code on Github[139].

Conclusion

Adding environment variables is a necessary step for any truly professional Django project.
They take some getting used to but are invaluable for switching between local and production
environments as we'll do later on in the book. In the next chapter we'll fully configure our email
settings and add password reset functionality.

---

[139]https://github.com/wsvincent/djangoforprofessionals/tree/master/ch8-environment-variables

Chapter 9: Email

In this chapter we will fully configure email and add password change and password reset functionality. Currently emails are not actually sent to users. They are simply outputted to our command line console. We'll change that by signing up for a third-party email service, obtaining API keys, and updating our `settings.py` file. Django takes care of the rest.

So far all of our work–custom user model, `pages` app, static assets, authentication with `allauth`, and environment variables–could apply to almost *any* new project. After this chapter we will start building out the `Bookstore` site itself as opposed to foundational steps.

Custom Confirmation Emails

Let's sign up for a new user account to review the current user registration flow. Then we'll customize it. Make sure you are logged out and then navigate to the Sign Up page. I've chosen to use `testuser3@email.com` and `testpass123` as the password.

testuser3 Sign Up

Upon submission we are redirected to the homepage with a custom greeting *and* an email is sent to us within the command line console. You can see this by checking the logs with `docker-compose logs`.

To customize this email we first need to find the existing templates. Navigate over to the django-allauth source code on Github[140] and perform a search with a portion of the generated text. That leads to the discovery that there are in fact two files used: one for the subject line, `email_confirmation_subject.txt`, and one for the email body called `email_confirmation_-message.txt`.

To update both we'll override them by recreating the same structure of `django-allauth` which means making our own `email` directory within `templates/account` and then adding our own versions of the files there.

Command Line

```
$ mkdir templates/account/email
$ touch templates/account/email/email_confirmation_subject.txt
$ touch templates/account/email/email_confirmation_message.txt
```

Let's start with the subject line since it's the shorter of the two. Here is the default text from `django-allauth`.

email_confirmation_subject.txt

```
{% load i18n %}
{% autoescape off %}
{% blocktrans %}Please Confirm Your E-mail Address{% endblocktrans %}
{% endautoescape %}
```

The first line, `{% load i18n %}`, is to support Django's internationalization[141] functionality, the ability to support multiple languages. Then comes the Django template tag for autoescape[142]. By default it is "on" and protects against security issues like cross site scripting. But since we can trust the content of the text here, it is turned off.

Finally, we come to our text itself which is wrapped in blocktrans[143] template tags to support translations. Let's change the text to demonstrate that we can.

---

[140]https://github.com/pennersr/django-allauth
[141]https://docs.djangoproject.com/en/3.1/topics/i18n/
[142]https://docs.djangoproject.com/en/3.1/ref/templates/builtins/#autoescape
[143]https://docs.djangoproject.com/en/3.1/topics/i18n/translation/#std:templatetag-blocktrans

email_confirmation_subject.txt

```
{% load i18n %}
{% autoescape off %}
{% blocktrans %}Confirm Your Sign Up{% endblocktrans %}
{% endautoescape %}
```

Now turn to the email confirmation message itself. Here is the current default[144]:

email_confirmation_message.txt

```
{% load account %}{% user_display user as user_display %}{% load i18n %}\
{% autoescape off %}{% blocktrans with site_name=current_site.name\
  site_domain=current_site.domain %}\
Hello from {{ site_name }}!

You're receiving this e-mail because user {{ user_display }} has given\
yours as an e-mail address to connect their account.

To confirm this is correct, go to {{ activate_url }}
{% endblocktrans %}{% endautoescape %}
{% blocktrans with site_name=current_site.name\
  site_domain=current_site.domain %}
Thank you from {{ site_name }}!
{{ site_domain }}{% endblocktrans %}
```

> Note that backslashes \ are included for formatting but are not necessary in the raw code. In other words, you can remove them from the code below–and other code examples–as needed.

You probably noticed that the default email sent referred to our site as example.com which is displayed here as {{ site_name }}. Where does that come from? The answer is the sites section of the Django admin, which is used by django-allauth. So head to the admin at http://127.0.0.1:8000/admin/ and click on the Sites link on the homepage.

---

[144]https://github.com/pennersr/django-allauth/blob/41f84f5530b75431cfd4cf2b89cd805ced009e7d/allauth/templates/account/email/email_confirmation_message.txt

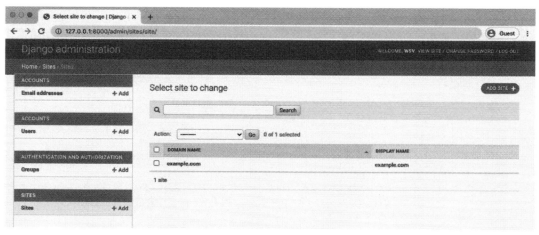

Admin Sites

There is a "Domain Name" and a "Display Name" here. Click on example.com under "Domain Name" so we can edit it. The Domain Name[145] is the full domain name for a site, for example it might be djangobookstore.com, while the Display Name[146] is a human-readable name for the site such as Django Bookstore.

Make these updates and click the "Save" button in the lower right corner when done.

Admin Sites – DjangoBookstore.com

---

[145]https://docs.djangoproject.com/en/3.1/ref/contrib/sites/#django.contrib.sites.models.Site.domain
[146]https://docs.djangoproject.com/en/3.1/ref/contrib/sites/#django.contrib.sites.models.Site.name

Ok, back to our email. Let's customize it a bit by changing the greeting from "Hello" to "Hi".

email_confirmation_message.txt

```
{% load account %}{% user_display user as user_display %}{% load i18n %}\
{% autoescape off %}{% blocktrans with site_name=current_site.name
  \site_domain=current_site.domain %}
Hi from {{ site_name }}!

You're receiving this e-mail because user {{ user_display }} has given\
yours as an e-mail address to connect their account.

To confirm this is correct, go to {{ activate_url }}
{% endblocktrans %}{% endautoescape %}
{% blocktrans with site_name=current_site.name\
  site_domain=current_site.domain %}
Thank you from {{ site_name }}!
{{ site_domain }}{% endblocktrans %}
```

One final item to change. Did you notice the email was from `webmaster@localhost`? That's a default setting we can also update via DEFAULT_FROM_EMAIL[147]. Let's do that now by adding the following line at the bottom of the `config/settings.py` file.

Code

```
# config/settings.py
DEFAULT_FROM_EMAIL = 'admin@djangobookstore.com'
```

Make sure you are logged out of the site and go to the Sign Up page again to create a new user. I've used `testuser4@email.com` for convenience.

[147]https://docs.djangoproject.com/en/3.1/ref/settings/#default-from-email

Sign Up testuser4

Log in and after being redirected to the homepage check the command line to see the message by typing `docker-compose logs`.

Command Line

```
...
web_1  |  Content-Transfer-Encoding: 7bit
web_1  |  Subject: [Django Bookstore] Confirm Your Sign Up
web_1  |  From: admin@djangobookstore.com
web_1  |  To: testuser4@email.com
web_1  |  Date: Mon, 03 Aug 2020 18:34:50 -0000
web_1  |  Message-ID: <156312929025.27.2332096239397833769@87d045aff8f7>
web_1  |
web_1  |  Hi from Django Bookstore!
web_1  |
web_1  |  You're receiving this e-mail because user testuser4 has given yours\
as an e-mail address to connect their account.
web_1  |
web_1  |  To confirm this is correct, go to http://127.0.0.1:8000/accounts/\
confirm-email/NA:1hmjKk:6MiDB5XoLW3HAhePuZ5WucR0Fiw/
web_1  |
web_1  |  Thank you from Django Bookstore!
web_1  |  djangobookstore.com
```

And there it is with the new `From` setting, the new domain `djangobookstore.com`, and the new message in the email.

Email Confirmation Page

Click on the unique URL link in the email which redirects to the email confirm page.

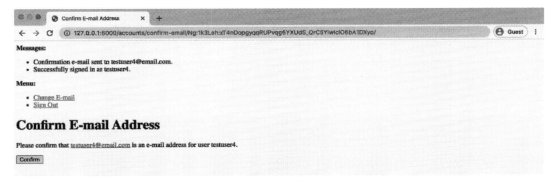

Confirm Email Page

Not very attractive. Let's update it to match the look of the rest of our site. Searching again in the django-allauth source code on Github[148] reveals the name and location of this file is `templates/account/email_confirm.html`. So let's create our own template.

Command Line

```
$ touch templates/account/email_confirm.html
```

And then update it to extend `_base.html` and use Bootstrap for the button.

---

[148]https://github.com/pennersr/django-allauth

Code

```
<!-- templates/account/email_confirm.html -->
{% extends '_base.html' %}
{% load i18n %}
{% load account %}

{% block head_title %}{% trans "Confirm E-mail Address" %}{% endblock %}

{% block content %}
  <h1>{% trans "Confirm E-mail Address" %}</h1>
  {% if confirmation %}
    {% user_display confirmation.email_address.user as user_display %}
    <p>{% blocktrans with confirmation.email_address.email as email %}Please confirm
that <a href="mailto:{{ email }}">{{ email }}</a> is an e-mail address for user
{{ user_display }}.{% endblocktrans %}</p>
    <form method="post" action="{% url 'account_confirm_email' confirmation.key %}">
{% csrf_token %}
      <button class="btn btn-primary" type="submit">{% trans 'Confirm' %}</button>
    </form>
  {% else %}
    {% url 'account_email' as email_url %}
    <p>{% blocktrans %}This e-mail confirmation link expired or is invalid. Please
    <a href="{{ email_url }}">issue a new e-mail confirmation request</a>.\
    {% endblocktrans %}</p>
  {% endif %}
{% endblock %}
```

Refresh the page to see our update.

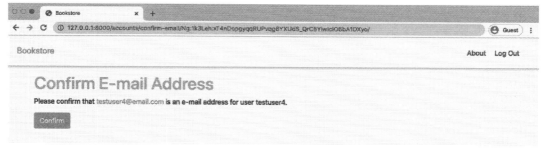

Confirm Email Page Updated

Password Reset and Password Change

Django and `django-allauth` also come with support for additional user account features such as the ability to reset a forgotten password and change your existing password if already logged in.

The locations of the default password reset and password change pages are as follows:

- `http://127.0.0.1:8000/accounts/password/reset/`
- `http://127.0.0.1:8000/accounts/password/change/`

If you go through the flow of each you can find the corresponding templates and email messages in the `django-allauth` source code.

Email Service

The emails we have configured so far are generally referred to as "Transactional Emails" as they occur based on a user action of some kind. This is in contrast to "Marketing Emails" such as, say, a monthly newsletter.

There are many transactional email providers available including SendGrid, MailGun, Amazon's Simple Email Service. Django is agnostic about which provider is used; the steps are similar for all and many have a free tier available.

After signing up for an account with your email service of choice you'll often have a choice between using SMTP[149] or a Web API. SMTP is easier to configure, but a web API is more configurable and robust. Start with SMTP and work your way from there: email configurations can be quite complex in their own right.

After obtaining a username and password with an email provider, a few settings tweaks will allow Django to use them to send emails.

The first step would be to update the `EMAIL_BACKEND` config, which should be near the bottom of the `config/settings.py` file since we previously updated it.

---

[149]https://en.wikipedia.org/wiki/Simple_Mail_Transfer_Protocol

Code

```
# config/settings.py
EMAIL_BACKEND = 'django.core.mail.backends.smtp.EmailBackend' # new
```

And then to configure `EMAIL_HOST`, `EMAIL_HOST_USER`, `EMAIL_HOST_PASSWORD`, `EMAIL_PORT`, and `EMAIL_USE_TLS` based on the instructions from your email provider as environment variables.

In the official source code the `EMAIL_BACKEND` will remain `console`, but the previous steps are how to add an email service. If you find yourself frustrated properly configuring email, well, you're not alone! Django does at least make it far, far easier than implementing without the benefits of a batteries-included framework.

Git

To commit this chapter's code updates make sure to check the status of changes, add them all, and include a commit message.

Command Line

```
$ git status
$ git add .
$ git commit -m 'ch9'
```

If you have any issues compare your code against the official source code on Github[150].

Conclusion

Configuring email properly is largely a one-time pain. But it is a necessary part of any production website. This concludes the foundational chapters for our Bookstore project. In the next chapter we'll finally start building out the Bookstore itself.

---

[150]https://github.com/wsvincent/djangoforprofessionals/tree/master/ch9-email

Chapter 10: Books App

In this chapter we will build a *Books* app for our project that displays all available books and has an individual page for each. We'll also explore different URL approaches starting with using an id, then switching to a slug, and finally using a UUID.

To start, we must create this new app which we'll call books.

Command Line

```
$ docker-compose exec web python manage.py startapp books
```

And to ensure Django knows about our new app, open your text editor and add the new app to INSTALLED_APPS in our config/settings.py file:

Code

```python
# config/settings.py
INSTALLED_APPS = [
    'django.contrib.admin',
    'django.contrib.auth',
    'django.contrib.contenttypes',
    'django.contrib.sessions',
    'django.contrib.messages',
    'django.contrib.staticfiles',
    'django.contrib.sites',

    # Third-party
    'allauth',
    'allauth.account',
    'crispy_forms',

    # Local
    'accounts',
    'pages',
    'books', # new
]
```

Ok, initial creation complete!

Models

Ultimately we'll need a model, view, url, and template for each page so it's common to debate where to start. The model is a good place to start as it sets the structure. Let's think about what fields we might want to include. To keep things simple we'll start with a `title`, `author`, and `price`.

Update the `books/models.py` file to include our new `Books` model.

Code

```
# books/models.py
from django.db import models


class Book(models.Model):
    title = models.CharField(max_length=200)
    author = models.CharField(max_length=200)
    price = models.DecimalField(max_digits=6, decimal_places=2)

    def __str__(self):
        return self.title
```

At the top we're importing the Django class `models` and then creating a `Book` model that subclasses it which means we automatically have access to everything within django.db.models.Model[151] and can add additional fields and methods as desired.

For `title` and `author` we're limiting the length to 200 characters and for `price` using a DecimalField[152] which is a good choice when dealing with currency.

Below we've specified a `__str__` method to control how the object is outputted in the Admin and Django shell.

Now that our new database model is created we need to create a new migration record for it.

---

[151]https://docs.djangoproject.com/en/3.1/topics/db/models/
[152]https://docs.djangoproject.com/en/3.1/ref/models/fields/#decimalfield

Command Line

```
$ docker-compose exec web python manage.py makemigrations books
Migrations for 'books':
  books/migrations/0001_initial.py
    - Create model Book
```

And then apply the migration to our database.

Command Line

```
$ docker-compose exec web python manage.py migrate
```

Adding the name of the app books to each command is optional but a good habit as it keeps both the migrations file and the migrate command focused on just that app. If we'd left the app name off then all changes would be included in the migrations file and database migrate which can be harder to debug later on.

Our database is configured. Let's add some data to the admin.

Admin

We need a way to access our data for which the Django admin is perfectly suited. Don't forget to update the books/admin.py file or else the app won't appear! I forget this step almost every time even after using Django for years.

Code

```
# books/admin.py
from django.contrib import admin
from .models import Book

admin.site.register(Book)
```

If you look into the admin at http://127.0.0.1:8000/admin/ the Books app is now there.

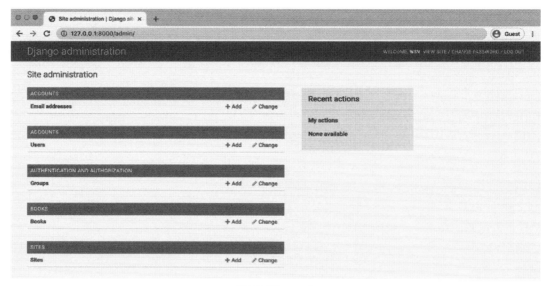

Admin Homepage

Let's add a book entry for *Django for Professionals*. Click on the + Add button next to Books to create a new entry. The title is "Django for Professionals", the author is "William S. Vincent", and the price is $39.00. There's no need to include the dollar sign $ in the amount as we'll add that in our eventual template.

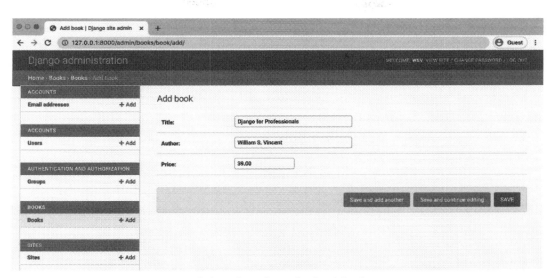

Admin - Django for Professionals book

After clicking on the "Save" button it redirects to the main Books page which only shows the title.

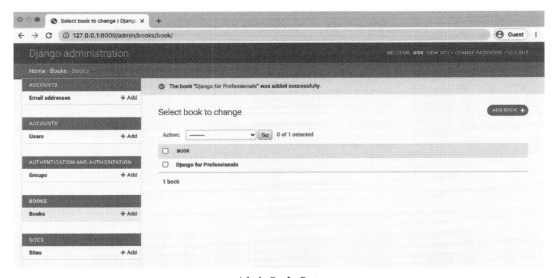

Admin Books Page

Let's update the books/admin.py file to specify which fields we also want displayed.

Code

```
# books/admin.py
from django.contrib import admin
from .models import Book

class BookAdmin(admin.ModelAdmin):
    list_display = ("title", "author", "price",)

admin.site.register(Book, BookAdmin)
```

Then refresh the page.

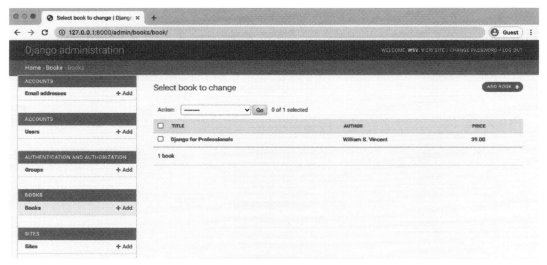

Admin Books List Page

Now that our database model is complete we need to create the necessary views, URLs, and templates so we can display the information on our web application. Where to start is always a question and a confusing one at that for developers.

Personally I often start with the URLs, then the Views, and the Templates.

URLs

We need to update two urls.py files. The first one is config/urls.py. Add the new path for the books app.

Code

```
# config/urls.py
from django.contrib import admin
from django.urls import path, include

urlpatterns = [
    # Django admin
    path('admin/', admin.site.urls),

    # User management
    path('accounts/', include('allauth.urls')),

    # Local apps
    path('', include('pages.urls')),
    path('books/', include('books.urls')), # new
]
```

Now create our books app URLs paths. We must create this file first.

Command Line

```
$ touch books/urls.py
```

We'll use empty string `''` so combined with the fact that all books app URLs will start at books/ that will also be the route for our main list view of each book. The view it references, BookListView, has yet to be created.

Code

```
# books/urls.py
from django.urls import path
from .views import BookListView

urlpatterns = [
    path('', BookListView.as_view(), name='book_list'),
]
```

Views

Moving on time for that BookListView we just referenced in our URLs file. This will rely on the built-in ListView[153], a Generic Class-Based View provided for common use cases like this. All we must do is specify the proper model and template to be used.

Code

```
# books/views.py
from django.views.generic import ListView
from .models import Book


class BookListView(ListView):
    model = Book
    template_name = 'books/book_list.html'
```

Note the template book_list.html does not exist yet.

Templates

It is optional to create an app specific folder within templates but it can help especially as number grows in size so we'll create one called books.

---

[153]https://docs.djangoproject.com/en/3.1/ref/class-based-views/generic-display/#django.views.generic.list. ListView

Command Line

```
$ mkdir templates/books/
$ touch templates/books/book_list.html
```

Code

```
<!-- templates/books/book_list.html -->
{% extends '_base.html' %}

{% block title %}Books{% endblock title %}

{% block content %}
  {% for book in object_list %}
    <div>
      <h2><a href="">{{ book.title }}</a></h2>
    </div>
  {% endfor %}
{% endblock content %}
```

At the top we note that this template extends _base.html and then wraps our desired code with content blocks. We use the Django Templating Language to set up a simple *for loop* for each book. Note that object_list comes from ListView and contains all the objects in our view.

The final step is to spin up and then down our containers to reload the Django settings.py file. Otherwise it won't realize we've made a change and so there will be an error page and in the logs a message about "ModuleNotFoundError: No module named 'books.urls'".

Spin down and then up again our containers.

Command Line

```
$ docker-compose down
$ docker-compose up -d
```

If you go to http://127.0.0.1:8000/books/ now the books page will work.

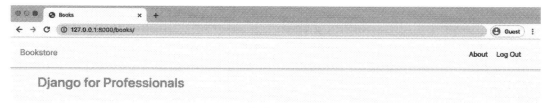

Books Page

object_list

ListView relies on `object_list`, as we just saw, but this is far from descriptive. A better approach is to rename it to a friendlier[154] name using `context_object_name`.

Update `books/views.py` as follows.

Code

```
# books/views.py
from django.views.generic import ListView
from .models import Book


class BookListView(ListView):
    model = Book
    context_object_name = 'book_list' # new
    template_name = 'books/book_list.html'
```

And then swap out `object_list` in our template for `book_list`.

---

[154]https://docs.djangoproject.com/en/3.1/topics/class-based-views/generic-display/#making-friendly-template-contexts

Code

```
<!-- templates/books/book_list.html -->
{% extends '_base.html' %}

{% block title %}Books{% endblock title %}

{% block content %}
  {% for book in book_list %}
    <div>
      <h2><a href="">{{ book.title }}</a></h2>
    </div>
  {% endfor %}
{% endblock content %}
```

Refresh the page and it will still work as before! This technique is especially helpful on larger projects where multiple developers are working on a project. It's hard for a front-end engineer to guess correctly what `object_list` means!

To prove the list view works for multiple items add two more books to the site via the admin. I've added my two other Django books–*Django for Beginners* and *Django for APIs*–which both have "William S. Vincent" as the author and "39.00" as the price.

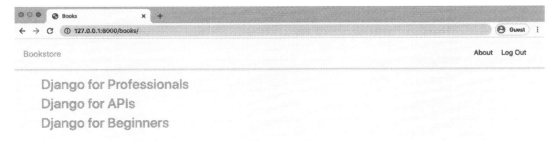

Three Books

Individual Book Page

Now we can add individual pages for each book by using another Generic Class-Based View called DetailView[155].

---

[155]https://docs.djangoproject.com/en/3.1/ref/class-based-views/generic-display/#detailview

Our process is similar to the Books page and starts with the URL importing `BookDetailView`
on the second line and then setting the path to be the primary key of each book which will be
represented as an integer `<int:pk>`.

Code

```python
# books/urls.py
from django.urls import path
from .views import BookListView, BookDetailView # new

urlpatterns = [
    path('', BookListView.as_view(), name='book_list'),
    path('<int:pk>/', BookDetailView.as_view(), name='book_detail'), # new
]
```

Django automatically adds an auto-incrementing primary key[156] to our database models. So while
we only declared the fields `title`, `author`, and `body` on our `Book` model, under-the-hood Django
also added another field called `id`, which is our primary key. We can access it as either `id` or `pk`.

The `pk` for our first book is 1. For the second one it will 2. And so on. Therefore when we go to
the individual entry page for our first book, we can expect that its URL route will be `books/1`.

Now on to the `books/views.py` file where we'll import `DetailView` and create a `BookDetailView`
class that also specifies `model` and `template_name` fields.

Code

```python
# books/views.py
from django.views.generic import ListView, DetailView # new
from .models import Book


class BookListView(ListView):
    model = Book
    context_object_name = 'book_list'
    template_name = 'books/book_list.html'


class BookDetailView(DetailView): # new
    model = Book
    template_name = 'books/book_detail.html'
```

---

[156]https://docs.djangoproject.com/en/3.1/topics/db/models/#automatic-primary-key-fields

And finally the template `book_detail.html`.

Command Line

```
$ touch templates/books/book_detail.html
```

Then have it display all the current fields. We can also showcase the title in the `title` tags so that it appears in the web browser tab.

Code

```
<!-- templates/books/book_detail.html -->
{% extends '_base.html' %}

{% block title %}{{ object.title }}{% endblock title %}

{% block content %}
  <div class="book-detail">
    <h2><a href="">{{ object.title }}</a></h2>
    <p>Author: {{ object.author }}</p>
    <p>Price: {{ object.price }}</p>
  </div>
{% endblock content %}
```

If you navigate now to `http://127.0.0.1:8000/books/1/` you'll see a dedicated page for our first book.

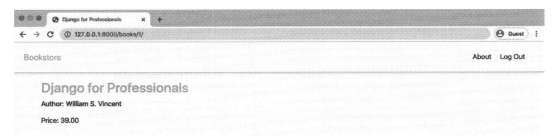

Book Detail Page

context_object_name

Just as `ListView` defaults to `object_list` which we updated to be more specific, so too `DetailView` defaults to `object` which we can make more descriptive using `context_object_name`.

We'll set it to book.

Code

```
# books/views.py
...
class BookDetailView(DetailView):
    model = Book
    context_object_name = 'book' # new
    template_name = 'books/book_detail.html'
```

Don't forget to update our template too with this change, swapping out `object` for `book` for our three fields.

Code

```
<!-- templates/books/book_detail.html -->
{% extends '_base.html' %}

{% block title %}{{ book.title }}{% endblock title %}

{% block content %}
  <div class="book-detail">
    <h2><a href="">{{ book.title }}</a></h2>
    <p>Author: {{ book.author }}</p>
    <p>Price: {{ book.price }}</p>
  </div>
{% endblock content %}
```

As a final step, we want the link on the book list page to point to an individual page. With the url template tag[157] we can point to `book_detail` – the URL name set in `books/urls.py` – and then pass in the `pk`.

---

[157]https://docs.djangoproject.com/en/3.1/ref/templates/builtins/#url

Code

```
<!-- templates/books/book_list.html -->
{% extends '_base.html' %}

{% block title %}Books{% endblock title %}

{% block content %}
  {% for book in book_list %}
    <div>
      <h2><a href="{% url 'book_detail' book.pk %}">{{ book.title }}</a></h2>
    </div>
  {% endfor %}
{% endblock content %}
```

Refresh the book list page at `http://127.0.0.1:8000/books/` and links are now all clickable and direct to the correct individual book page.

get_absolute_url

One additional step we haven't made yet is to add a get_absolute_url()[158] method which sets a canonical URL for the model. It is also required when using the reverse()[159] function, which is commonly used.

Here's how to add it to our `books/models.py` file. Import `reverse` at the top. Then add the `get_absolute_url` method which will be the reverse of our URL name, `book_detail`, and passes in the `id` as a string.

---

[158]https://docs.djangoproject.com/en/3.1/ref/models/instances/#get-absolute-url
[159]https://docs.djangoproject.com/en/3.1/ref/urlresolvers/#django.urls.reverse

Code

```python
# books/models.py
from django.db import models
from django.urls import reverse # new


class Book(models.Model):
    title = models.CharField(max_length=200)
    author = models.CharField(max_length=200)
    price = models.DecimalField(max_digits=6, decimal_places=2)

    def __str__(self):
        return self.title

    def get_absolute_url(self): # new
        return reverse('book_detail', args=[str(self.id)])
```

Then we can update the templates. Currently our a `href` link is using `{% url 'book_detail' book.pk %}`. However we can instead use `get_absolute_url` directly which already has the `pk` passed in.

Code

```html
<!-- templates/books/book_list.html -->
{% extends '_base.html' %}

{% block title %}Books{% endblock title %}

{% block content %}
  {% for book in book_list %}
    <div>
      <h2><a href="{{ book.get_absolute_url }}">{{ book.title }}</a></h2>
    </div>
  {% endfor %}
{% endblock content %}
```

There's no need to use the `url` template tag either, just one canonical reference that can be changed, if needed, in the `books/models.py` file and will propagate throughout the project from there. This is a cleaner approach and should be used whenever you need individual pages for an object.

Primary Keys vs. IDs

It can be confusing whether to use a primary key (PK) or an ID in a project, especially since Django's `DetailView` treats them interchangeably. However there is a subtle difference.

The `id` is a model field automatically set by Django internally to auto-increment. So the first book has an `id` of 1, the second entry of 2, and so on. This is also, by default, treated as the primary key `pk` of a model.

However it's possible to manually change what the primary key is for a model. It doesn't have to be `id`, but could be something like `object_id` depending on the use case. Additionally Python has a built-in id()[160] object which can sometimes cause confusion and/or bugs.

By contrast the primary key `pk` refers to the primary key field of a model so you're safer using `pk` when in doubt. And in fact in the next section we will update the `id` of our model!

Slugs vs. UUIDs

Using the `pk` field in the URL of our `DetailView` is quick and easy, but not ideal for a real-world project. The `pk` is currently the same as our auto-incrementing `id`. Among other concerns, it tells a potential hacker *exactly* how many records you have in your database; it tells them exactly what the `id` is which can be used in a potential attack; and there can be synchronization issues if you have multiple front-ends.

There are two alternative approaches. The first is called a "slug," a newspaper term for a short label for something that is often used in URLs. For example, in our example of "Django for Professionals" its slug could be `django-for-professionals`. There's even a SlugField[161] model field that can be used and either added when creating the `title` field by hand or auto-populated upon save. The main challenge with slugs is handling duplicates, though this can be solved by adding random strings or numbers to a given slug field. The synchronization issue remains though.

A better approach is to use a UUID (Universally Unique IDentifier)[162] which Django now supports

---

[160]https://docs.python.org/3/library/functions.html#id

[161]https://docs.djangoproject.com/en/3.1/ref/models/fields/#slugfield

[162]https://docs.python.org/3/library/uuid.html?highlight=uuid#module-uuid

via a dedicated UUIDField[163].

Let's implement a UUID now by adding a new field to our model and then updating the URL path.

Import uuid at the top and then update the id field to actually be a UUIDField that is now the primary key. We also use uuid4 for the encryption. This allows us to use DetailView which requires either a slug or pk field; it won't work with a UUID field without significant modification.

Code

```python
# books/models.py
import uuid # new
from django.db import models
from django.urls import reverse


class Book(models.Model):
    id = models.UUIDField( # new
        primary_key=True,
        default=uuid.uuid4,
        editable=False)
    title = models.CharField(max_length=200)
    author = models.CharField(max_length=200)
    price = models.DecimalField(max_digits=6, decimal_places=2)

    def __str__(self):
        return self.title

    def get_absolute_url(self):
        return reverse('book_detail', args=[str(self.id)])
```

In the URL path swap out int for uuid in the detail view.

---

[163]https://docs.djangoproject.com/en/3.1/ref/models/fields/#django.db.models.UUIDField

Code

```
# books/urls.py
from django.urls import path
from .views import BookListView, BookDetailView

urlpatterns = [
    path('', BookListView.as_view(), name='book_list'),
    path('<uuid:pk>', BookDetailView.as_view(), name='book_detail'), # new
]
```

But now we are faced with a problem: there are existing book entries, three in fact, with their own ids as well as related migration files that use them. Creating a new migration like this causes real problems[164]. The simplest approach, which we will use, is the most destructive: to simply delete old books migrations and start over.

Command Line

```
$ docker-compose exec web rm -r books/migrations
$ docker-compose down
```

One last issue is that we are also persisting our PostgreSQL database via a volume mount that still has records to the older id fields. You can see this with the docker volume ls command.

Command Line

```
$ docker volume ls
DRIVER              VOLUME NAME
local               books_postgres_data
```

The simplest approach is again to simply delete the volume and start over with Docker. As we're early enough in the project we'll take this route; a more mature project would require considering a more complex approach.

The steps involve starting up our web and db containers; adding a new initial migration file for the books app, applying all updates with migrate, and then creating a superuser account again.

---

[164]https://docs.djangoproject.com/en/3.1/howto/writing-migrations/#migrations-that-add-unique-fields

Command Line

```
$ docker volume rm books_postgres_data
$ docker-compose up -d
$ docker-compose exec web python manage.py makemigrations books
$ docker-compose exec web python manage.py migrate
$ docker-compose exec web python manage.py createsuperuser
```

Now go into admin and add the three books again. If you then navigate to the main books page
and click on an individual book you'll be taken to a new detail page with a UUID in the URL.

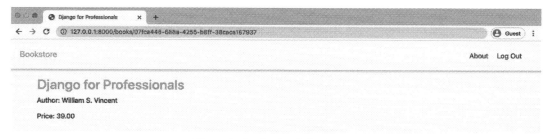

Django for Professionals book UUID

Navbar

Let's add a link to the books page in our navbar. We can use the url template tag and the URL
name of the page: book_list.

Code

```
<!-- templates/_base.html -->
<nav class="my-2 my-md-0 mr-md-3">
  <a class="p-2 text-dark" href="{% url 'book_list' %}">Books</a>
  <a class="p-2 text-dark" href="{% url 'about' %}">About</a>
```

Updated NavBar

Tests

We need to test our model and views now. We want to ensure that the `Books` model works as expected, including its `str` representation. And we want to test both `ListView` and `DetailView`.

Here's what sample tests look like in the `books/tests.py` file.

Code

```python
# books/tests.py
from django.test import TestCase
from django.urls import reverse
from .models import Book


class BookTests(TestCase):

    def setUp(self):
        self.book = Book.objects.create(
            title='Harry Potter',
            author='JK Rowling',
            price='25.00',
        )

    def test_book_listing(self):
        self.assertEqual(f'{self.book.title}', 'Harry Potter')
        self.assertEqual(f'{self.book.author}', 'JK Rowling')
        self.assertEqual(f'{self.book.price}', '25.00')

    def test_book_list_view(self):
        response = self.client.get(reverse('book_list'))
```

```
        self.assertEqual(response.status_code, 200)
        self.assertContains(response, 'Harry Potter')
        self.assertTemplateUsed(response, 'books/book_list.html')

    def test_book_detail_view(self):
        response = self.client.get(self.book.get_absolute_url())
        no_response = self.client.get('/books/12345/')
        self.assertEqual(response.status_code, 200)
        self.assertEqual(no_response.status_code, 404)
        self.assertContains(response, 'Harry Potter')
        self.assertTemplateUsed(response, 'books/book_detail.html')
```

We import `TestCase` and in our `setUp` method we add a sample book to test. `test_book_listing`
checks that both its string representation and content are correct. Then we use `test_book_-`
`list_view` to confirm that our homepage returns a 200 HTTP status code, contains our body
text, and uses the correct `books/book_list.html` template. Finally, `test_book_detail_view` tests
that our detail page works as expected and that an incorrect page returns a 404. It's always good
both to test that something **does** exist and that something incorrect **doesn't** exist in your tests.

Go ahead and run these tests now. They should all pass.

Command Line

```
$ docker-compose exec web python manage.py test
Creating test database for alias 'default'...
System check identified no issues (0 silenced).
.................
----------------------------------------------------------------------
Ran 17 tests in 0.369s

OK
Destroying test database for alias 'default'...
```

Git

We've done a lot of work in this chapter so add it all to version control now with Git by adding
new files and adding a commit message.

Command Line

```
$ git status
$ git add .
$ git commit -m 'ch10'
```

The official source code for this chapter is available on Github[165] for reference.

Conclusion

We're at the end of quite a long chapter, but the architecture of our Bookstore project is now much clearer. We've added a books model, learned how to change the URL structure, and switched to the much more secure UUID pattern.

In the next chapter we'll learn about foreign key relationships and add a reviews option to our project.

---

[165]https://github.com/wsvincent/djangoforprofessionals/tree/master/ch10-books

Chapter 11: Reviews App

In this chapter we'll add a `reviews` app so that readers can leave reviews of their favorite books. It gives us a chance to discuss foreign keys, app structure, and dive into forms.

Foreign Keys

We've already used a foreign key with our user model, but didn't have to think about it. Now we do! Fundamentally a database table can be thought of as similar to a spreadsheet with rows and columns. There needs to be a *primary key* field that is unique and refers to each record. In the last chapter we changed that from `id` to a `UUID`, but one still exists!

This matters when we want to link two tables together. For example, our `Books` model will link to a `Reviews` model since each review has to be connected to a relevant book. This implies a foreign key relationship.

There are three possible types of foreign key relationships:

- One-to-one[166]
- One-to-many[167]
- Many-to-many[168]

A `one-to-one` relationship is the simplest kind. An example would be a table of people's names and a table of social security numbers. Each person has only **one** social security number and each social security number is linked to only **one** person.

In practice `one-to-one` relationships are rare. It's unusual for both sides of a relationship to only be matched to one counterpart. Some other examples though would be country-flag or person-passport.

---

[166]https://docs.djangoproject.com/en/3.1/ref/models/fields/#onetoonefield
[167]https://docs.djangoproject.com/en/3.1/ref/models/fields/#foreignkey
[168]https://docs.djangoproject.com/en/3.1/ref/models/fields/#manytomanyfield

A one-to-many relationship is far more common and is the default foreign key[169] setting within Django. For example, **one** student can sign up for **many** classes. Or an employee has **one** job title, maybe "Software Engineer," but there can be **many** software engineers within a given company.

It's also possible to have a ManyToManyField[170] relationship. Let's consider a list of books and a list of authors: each book could have more than one author and each author can write more than one book. That's a many-to-many relationship. Just as with the previous two examples you need a linked Foreign Key field to connect the two lists. Additional examples include doctors and patients (every doctor sees multiple patients and vice versa) or employees and tasks (each employee has multiple tasks while each task is worked on by multiple employees).

Database design is a fascinating, deep topic that is both an art and a science. As the number of tables grow in a project over time it is almost inevitable that a refactoring will need to occur to address issues around inefficiency, bloat, and outright errors. Normalization[171] is the process of structuring a relational database though far beyond the scope of this book.

Reviews model

Coming back to our basic reviews app, the first consideration is what type of foreign key relationship will there be. If we are going to link a user to a review, then it is a straightforward one-to-many relationship. However it could also be possible to link books to reviews which would be many-to-many. The "correct" choice quickly becomes somewhat subjective and certainly dependent upon the particular needs of the project.

In this project we'll treat the reviews app as a one-to-many between authors and reviews as it's the simpler approach.

Here again we face a choice around how to design our project. Do we add the `Reviews` model within our existing `books/models.py` file or create a dedicated `reviews` app that we then link to? Let's start by adding a `Reviews` model to the `books` app.

---

[169]https://docs.djangoproject.com/en/3.1/ref/models/fields/#foreignkey
[170]https://docs.djangoproject.com/en/3.1/ref/models/fields/#manytomanyfield
[171]https://en.wikipedia.org/wiki/Database_normalization

Code

```python
# books/models.py
import uuid
from django.contrib.auth import get_user_model # new
from django.db import models
from django.urls import reverse


class Book(models.Model):
    ...


class Review(models.Model): # new
    book = models.ForeignKey(
        Book,
        on_delete=models.CASCADE,
        related_name='reviews',
    )
    review = models.CharField(max_length=255)
    author = models.ForeignKey(
        get_user_model(),
        on_delete=models.CASCADE,
    )

    def __str__(self):
        return self.review
```

At the top, under imports include `get_user_model`, which is needed to refer to our `CustomUser` model, then create a dedicated `Review` model. The `book` field is the one-to-many foreign key that links `Book` to `Review` and we're following the standard practice of naming it the same as the linked model. The `review` field contains the actual content which perhaps could be a TextField[172] depending on how much space you want to provide for review length! For now, we'll force reviews to be short at 255 characters or less. And then we'll *also* link to the `author` field to auto-populate the current user with the review.

For all many-to-one relationships such as a ForeignKey we must also specify an on_delete[173] option. And we're using get_user_model[174] to reference our custom user model.

[172]https://docs.djangoproject.com/en/3.1/ref/models/fields/#django.db.models.TextField
[173]https://docs.djangoproject.com/en/3.1/ref/models/fields/#django.db.models.ForeignKey.on_delete
[174]https://learndjango.com/tutorials/django-best-practices-referencing-user-model

Create a new migrations file for our changes and then run `migrate` to apply them.

Command Line

```
$ docker-compose exec web python manage.py makemigrations books
$ docker-compose exec web python manage.py migrate
```

Admin

For the reviews app to appear in the admin we need to update `books/admin.py` substantially by adding the `Review` model and specifying a display of TabularInline[175].

Code

```python
# books/admin.py
from django.contrib import admin
from .models import Book, Review

class ReviewInline(admin.TabularInline):
    model = Review

class BookAdmin(admin.ModelAdmin):
    inlines = [
        ReviewInline,
    ]
    list_display = ("title", "author", "price",)

admin.site.register(Book, BookAdmin)
```

Now navigate to the books section at `http://127.0.0.1:8000/admin/books/book/` and then click on any of the books to see the reviews visible on the individual book page.

---

[175]https://docs.djangoproject.com/en/3.1/ref/contrib/admin/#django.contrib.admin.TabularInline

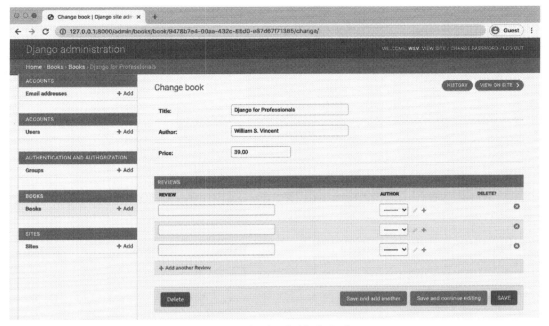

Django for Professionals Admin Reviews

We're limited to reviews by existing users at this point, although we have previously created a `testuser@email.com` that was deleted when we removed the database volume mount in the previous chapter. There are two options for adding this account: we could go to the main site and use the "Sign Up" link or we can add it directly from the admin. Let's do the latter. From the Users section on the Admin homepage click on the "+ Add" button. Add a new user called `testuser`.

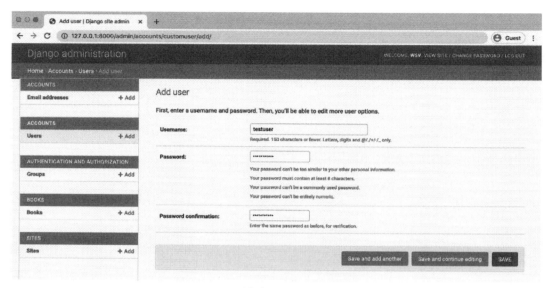

Admin testuser

Then on the next page add `testuser@email.com` as the email address. Scroll down to the bottom of the page and click the "Save" button.

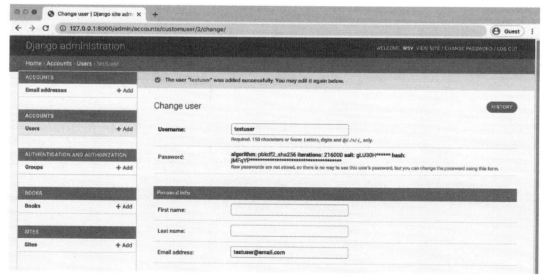

Admin testuser

Ok, finally, we can add reviews to the "Django for Professionals" book using `testuser`. Navigate back to the Books section and click on the correct book. Write two reviews and as AUTHOR make sure to select testuser.

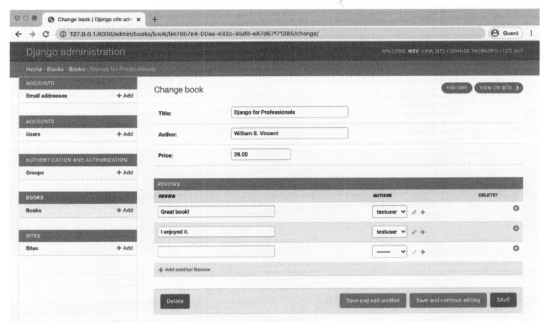

Add Two Reviews

Templates

With the reviews model set it's time to update our templates to display reviews on the individual page for each book. Add a basic "Reviews" section and then loop over all existing reviews. Since this is a foreign key relationship we follow it by using book.reviews.all. Then display the review field with review.review and the author with review.author.

Code

```
# templates/books/book_detail.html
{% extends '_base.html' %}

{% block title %}{{ book.title }}{% endblock title %}

{% block content %}
  <div class="book-detail">
    <h2><a href="">{{ book.title }}</a></h2>
    <p>Author: {{ book.author }}</p>
    <p>Price: {{ book.price }}</p>
    <div>
      <h3>Reviews</h3>
      <ul>
        {% for review in book.reviews.all %}
        <li>{{ review.review }} ({{ review.author }})</li>
        {% endfor %}
      </ul>
    </div>
  </div>
{% endblock content %}
```

That's it! Navigate over to the "Django for Professionals" individual page to see the result. Your url will be different than the one here because we're using a UUID.

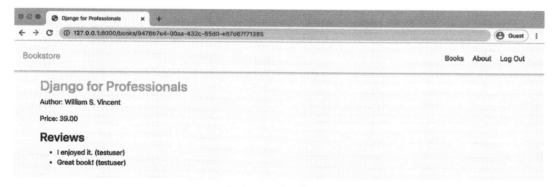

Reviews on Detail Page

Tests

Time for tests. We need to create a new user for our review and add a review to the setUp method in our test suite. Then we can test that the book object contains the correct review.

This involves importing get_user_model as well as adding the Review model at the top. We can use create_user to make a new user called reviewuser and then a review object that is linked to our single book object. Finally under test_book_detail_view we can add an additional assertContains test to the response object.

Code

```python
# books/tests.py
from django.contrib.auth import get_user_model # new
from django.test import TestCase
from django.urls import reverse
from .models import Book, Review # new


class BookTests(TestCase):

    def setUp(self):
        self.user = get_user_model().objects.create_user( # new
            username='reviewuser',
            email='reviewuser@email.com',
            password='testpass123'
        )

        self.book = Book.objects.create(
            title='Harry Potter',
            author='JK Rowling',
            price='25.00',
        )

        self.review = Review.objects.create( # new
            book = self.book,
            author = self.user,
            review = 'An excellent review',
        )

    def test_book_listing(self):
        self.assertEqual(f'{self.book.title}', 'Harry Potter')
        self.assertEqual(f'{self.book.author}', 'JK Rowling')
```

```
        self.assertEqual(f'{self.book.price}', '25.00')

    def test_book_list_view(self):
        response = self.client.get(reverse('book_list'))
        self.assertEqual(response.status_code, 200)
        self.assertContains(response, 'Harry Potter')
        self.assertTemplateUsed(response, 'books/book_list.html')

    def test_book_detail_view(self):
        response = self.client.get(self.book.get_absolute_url())
        no_response = self.client.get('/books/12345/')
        self.assertEqual(response.status_code, 200)
        self.assertEqual(no_response.status_code, 404)
        self.assertContains(response, 'Harry Potter')
        self.assertContains(response, 'An excellent review') # new
        self.assertTemplateUsed(response, 'books/book_detail.html')
```

If you run the tests now they all should pass.

Command Line

```
$ docker-compose exec web python manage.py test
Creating test database for alias 'default'...
System check identified no issues (0 silenced).
.................
----------------------------------------------------------------------
Ran 17 tests in 0.675s

OK
Destroying test database for alias 'default'...
```

Git

Add our new code changes to Git and include a commit message for the chapter.

Command Line

```
$ git status
$ git add .
$ git commit -m 'ch11'
```

The code for this chapter can be found on the official Github repository[176].

Conclusion

With more time we might update the reviews' functionality with a form on the page itself, however this means AJAX calls using jQuery, React, Vue, or another dedicated JavaScript framework. Unfortunately covering that fully is well beyond the scope of this book.

As the project grows it might also make sense to split reviews off into its own dedicated app. Doing so is a very subjective call. In general, keeping things as simple as possible–adding foreign keys within an existing app until it becomes too large to easily understand–is a solid approach.

In the next chapter we will add image uploads to our site so there can be covers for each book.

---

[176]https://github.com/wsvincent/djangoforprofessionals/tree/master/ch11-reviews

Chapter 12: File/Image Uploads

We previously configured static assets such as images in Chapter 6, but user-uploaded files, such as book covers, are somewhat different. To start with, Django refers to the former as `static` whereas anything uploaded by a user, whether it be a file or an image, is referred to as `media`.

The process for adding this feature for files or images is similar, but for images the Python image processing library Pillow[177] must be installed which includes additional features such as basic validation.

Let's install `pillow` using our by-now-familiar pattern of installing it within Docker, stopping our containers, and forcing a build of the new image.

Command Line

```
$ docker-compose exec web pipenv install pillow==7.2.0
$ docker-compose down
$ docker-compose up -d --build
```

Media Files

Fundamentally the difference between static and media files is that we can trust the former, but we definitely can't trust the latter by default. There are always security concerns[178] when dealing with user-uploaded content[179]. Notably, it's important to *validate all uploaded files* to ensure they are what they say they are. There are a number of nasty ways a malicious actor can attack a website that blindly accepts user uploads.

To start let's add two new configurations to the `config/settings.py` file. By default `MEDIA_URL` and `MEDIA_ROOT` are both empty and not displayed so we need to configure them:

---

[177] https://python-pillow.org/

[178] https://docs.djangoproject.com/en/3.1/ref/models/fields/#file-upload-security

[179] https://docs.djangoproject.com/en/3.1/topics/security/#user-uploaded-content

- MEDIA_ROOT[180] is the absolute file system path to the directory for user-uploaded files
- MEDIA_URL[181] is the URL we can use in our templates for the files

We can add both of these settings after `STATICFILES_FINDERS` near the bottom of the `config/settings.py` file. We'll use the common convention of calling both `media`. Don't forget to include the trailing slash `/` for `MEDIA_URL`!

Code

```
# config/settings.py
MEDIA_URL = '/media/' # new
MEDIA_ROOT = str(BASE_DIR.joinpath('media')) # new
```

Next add a new directory called `media` and a subdirectory called `covers` within it.

Command Line

```
$ mkdir media
$ mkdir media/covers
```

And finally, since user-uploaded content is assumed to exist in a production context, to see media items locally we need to update `config/urls.py` to show the files locally. This involves importing both `settings` and `static` at the top and then adding an additional line at the bottom.

Code

```
# config/urls.py
from django.conf import settings # new
from django.conf.urls.static import static # new
from django.contrib import admin
from django.urls import path, include

urlpatterns = [
    # Django admin
    path('admin/', admin.site.urls),

    # User management
    path('accounts/', include('allauth.urls')),
```

---

[180] https://docs.djangoproject.com/en/3.1/ref/settings/#media-root
[181] https://docs.djangoproject.com/en/3.1/ref/settings/#media-url

```
    # Local apps
    path('', include('pages.urls')),
    path('books/', include('books.urls')),
] + static(settings.MEDIA_URL, document_root=settings.MEDIA_ROOT) # new
```

Models

With our generic media configuration out of the way we can now turn to our models. To store these images we'll use Django's ImageField[182] which comes with some basic image processing validation included.

The name of the field is `cover` and we specify the location of the uploaded image will be in `MEDIA_ROOT/covers` (the `MEDIA_ROOT` part is implied based on our earlier `settings.py` config).

Code

```
# books/models.py
class Book(models.Model):
    id = models.UUIDField(
        primary_key=True,
        default=uuid.uuid4,
        editable=False)
    title = models.CharField(max_length=200)
    author = models.CharField(max_length=200)
    price = models.DecimalField(max_digits=6, decimal_places=2)
    cover = models.ImageField(upload_to='covers/') # new

    def __str__(self):
        return self.title

    def get_absolute_url(self):
        return reverse('book_detail', kwargs={'pk': str(self.pk)})
```

If we wanted to allow uploads of a regular file rather than an image file the only difference

---

[182]https://docs.djangoproject.com/en/3.1/ref/models/fields/#django.db.models.ImageField

> could be to change `ImageField` to `FileField`.

Since we've updated the model it's time to create a migrations file.

Command Line

```
$ docker-compose exec web python manage.py makemigrations books
You are trying to add a non-nullable field 'cover_image' to book
without a default; we can't do that (the database needs something to populate
existing rows).
Please select a fix:
 1) Provide a one-off default now (will be set on all existing rows with a
    null value for this column)
 2) Quit, and let me add a default in models.py
Select an option:
```

Oops! What happened? We're adding a new database field, but we already have three entries in our database for each book. Yet we failed to set a default value for `cover`.

To fix this type 2 to quit and we'll add a blank[183] field set to `True` for existing images.

Code

```
# books/models.py
cover = models.ImageField(upload_to='covers/', blank=True) # new
```

> It's common to see `blank` and null[a] used together to set a default value on a field. A gotcha is that the *field type* – `ImageField` vs. `CharField` and so on – dictates how to use them properly so closely read the documentation for future use.
>
> [a]https://docs.djangoproject.com/en/3.1/ref/models/fields/#null

Now we can create a migrations file without errors.

---

[183]https://docs.djangoproject.com/en/3.1/ref/models/fields/#blank

Command Line

```
$ docker-compose exec web python manage.py makemigrations books
```

And then apply the migration to our database.

Command Line

```
$ docker-compose exec web python manage.py migrate
```

Admin

We're in the home stretch now! Navigate over to the admin and to the entry for the book "Django for Professionals." The cover field is visible already and we already have a copy of it locally within static/images/dfp.jpg so use that file for the upload and then click the "Save" button in bottom right.

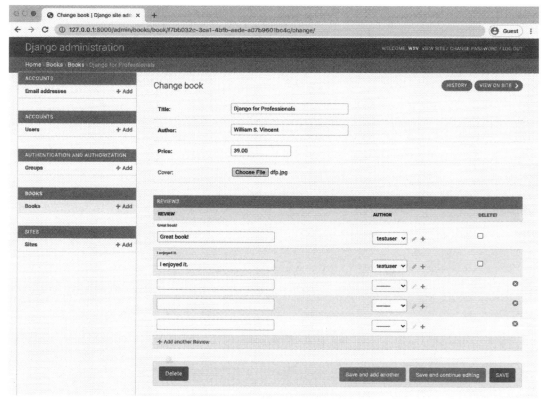

Admin add cover

This will redirect back to the main Books section. Click on the link again for "Django for Profesionals" and we can see it currently exists in our desired location of covers/.

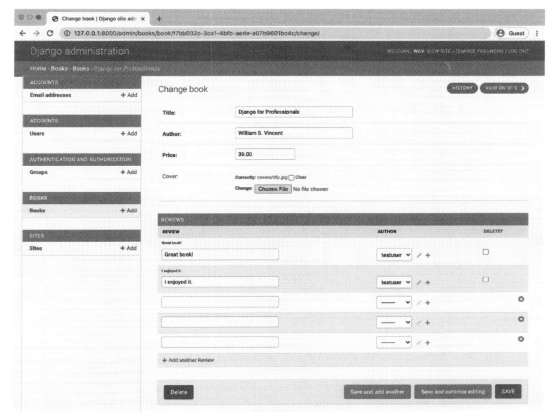

Admin with cover

Template

OK, final step. Let's update our template to display the book cover on the individual page. The route will be book.cover.url pointing to the location of the cover in our file system.

Here's what the updated book_detail.html file looks like with this one line change above the title.

Code

```
# templates/books/book_detail.html
{% extends '_base.html' %}

{% block title %}{{ book.title }}{% endblock title %}

{% block content %}
  <div class="book-detail">
    <img class="bookcover" src="{{ book.cover.url}}" alt="{{ book.title }}">
    <h2><a href="">{{ book.title }}</a></h2>
    <p>Author: {{ book.author }}</p>
    <p>Price: {{ book.price }}</p>
    <div>
      <h3>Reviews</h3>
      <ul>
        {% for review in book.reviews.all %}
        <li>{{ review.review }} ({{ review.author }})</li>
        {% endfor %}
      </ul>
    </div>
  </div>
{% endblock content %}
```

If you now visit the page for "Django for Professionals" you'll see the cover image proudly there!

Cover image

One potential gotcha is that our template now expects a `cover` to be present. If you navigate to either of the two other books, for which we have not added a cover, you'll see the following error message.

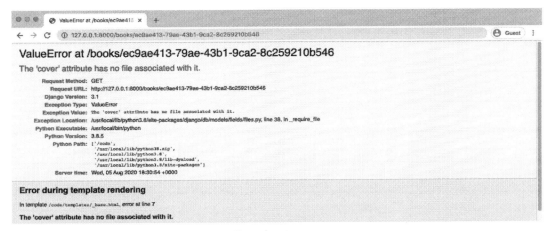

Cover image error

We must add some basic logic to our template so that if a cover is not present the template doesn't look for it! This can be done using an `if` statement that checks for `book.cover` and displays it if it exists.

Code

```
# templates/books/book_detail.html
{% extends '_base.html' %}

{% block title %}{{ book.title }}{% endblock title %}

{% block content %}
  <div class="book-detail">
    {% if book.cover %}
      <img class="bookcover" src="{{ book.cover.url}}" alt="{{ book.title }}">
    {% endif %}
    <h2><a href="">{{ book.title }}</a></h2>
  ...
```

If you refresh either book page now you'll see they display the correct page albeit without a cover.

Next Steps

There are several additional steps that might be nice to take in a project, but are beyond the scope of this book. These include adding dedicated create/edit/delete forms for the creation of books and cover image. A quite lengthy list of extra validations can and should be placed on the image-uploading form to ensure that only a normal image is added to the database.

A further step would be to store `media` files in a dedicated CDN (Content Delivery Network) for additional security. This can also be helpful for performance on very large sites for `static` files, but for `media` files is a good idea regardless of the size.

Finally tests would be nice to have here although they would be primarily focused on the form validation section, not the basic image-uploading via the admin. Again this is an area that can become quite complex, but is worthy of further study.

Git

Make sure to create a new Git commit for the changes in this chapter.

Command Line

```
$ git status
$ git add .
$ git commit -m 'ch12'
```

As always you can compare your code against the official source code on Github[184].

Conclusion

This chapter demonstrated how to add user files to a project. In practice it is straightforward, but the additional layer of security concerns makes it an area worthy of focus at scale.

In the next chapter we will add permissions to our site to lock it down.

[184] https://github.com/wsvincent/djangoforprofessionals/tree/master/ch12-file-image-uploads

Chapter 13: Permissions

Currently there are no permissions set on our Bookstore project. Any user, even one not logged in, can visit any page and perform any available action. While this is fine for prototyping, implementing a robust permissions structure is a must before deploying a website to production.

Django comes with built-in authorization options[185] for locking down pages to either logged in users, specific groups, or users with the proper individual permission.

Logged-In Users Only

Confusingly there are multiple ways to add even the most basic permission: restricting access only to logged-in users. It can be done in a raw way[186] using the login_required()[187] decorator, or since we are using class-based views so far via the LoginRequired mixin[188].

Let's start by limiting access to the Books pages only to logged-in users. There is a link for it in the navbar so this is not the case of a user accidentally finding a URL (which also can happen); in this case the URL is quite public.

First import `LoginRequiredMixin` at the top and then add it *before* `ListView` since mixins are loaded from left-to-right. That way the first thing that is checked is whether the user is logged in; if they're not there's no need to load the `ListView`. The other part is setting a `login_url` for the user to be redirected to. This is the URL name for log in which, since we're using `django-allauth` is `account_login`. If we were using the traditional Django authentication system then this link would be called simply `login`.

The structure for `BookDetailView` is the same: add `LoginRequiredMixin` and a `login_url` route.

---

[185]https://docs.djangoproject.com/en/3.1/topics/auth/default/#permissions-and-authorization
[186]https://docs.djangoproject.com/en/3.1/topics/auth/default/#the-raw-way
[187]https://docs.djangoproject.com/en/3.1/topics/auth/default/#the-login-required-decorator
[188]https://docs.djangoproject.com/en/3.1/topics/auth/default/#the-loginrequired-mixin

Code

```
# books/views.py
from django.contrib.auth.mixins import LoginRequiredMixin # new
from django.views.generic import ListView, DetailView
from .models import Book


class BookListView(LoginRequiredMixin, ListView): # new
    model = Book
    context_object_name = 'book_list'
    template_name = 'books/book_list.html'
    login_url = 'account_login' # new


class BookDetailView(LoginRequiredMixin, DetailView): # new
    model = Book
    context_object_name = 'book'
    template_name = 'books/book_detail.html'
    login_url = 'account_login' # new
```

And that's it! If you now log out of your account and click on the "Books" link it will automatically redirect you to the Log In page. However if you are logged in, the Books page loads normally.

Even if you somehow knew the UUID of a specific book page you'd be redirected to Log In as well!

Permissions

Django comes with a basic permissions system[189] that is controlled through the Django admin. To demonstrate it we need to create a new user account. Navigate back to the Admin homepage and then click on "+ Add" next to Users.

We'll call this new user special and set a password of testpass123. Click on the "Save" button.

---

[189]https://docs.djangoproject.com/en/3.1/topics/auth/default/#permissions-and-authorization

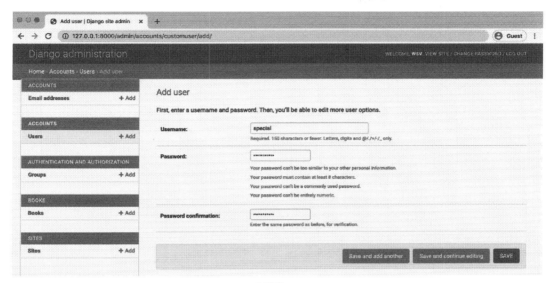

Add User

The second page allows us to set an "Email address" to special@email.com. We're using django-allauth so that our log in page requires only email and the sign up page also only uses email, but since we didn't customize the admin as well it still expects a username when creating a new user this way.

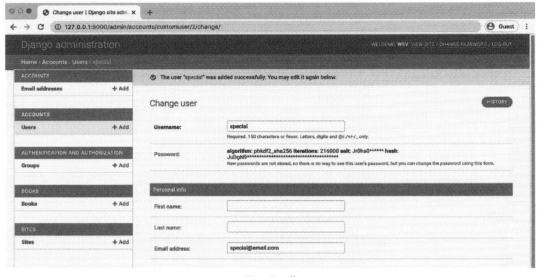

User Email

> If we *had* wanted to fully rip out the default user system that would mean using Abstract-
> BaseUser[a] rather than AbstractUser back in Chapter 3 when we configured our custom user
> model.
>
> [a]https://docs.djangoproject.com/en/3.1/topics/auth/customizing/#django.contrib.auth.models.
> AbstractBaseUser

Scrolling down further on the page to the bottom there are options to set Groups as well as User
permissions. This is a long list of defaults Django provides. For now we won't use them since we'll
create a custom permission in the next section so just click on the "Save" button in the lower
right corner so that our email address is updated for the user account.

Custom Permissions

Setting custom permissions[190] is a much more common occurrence in a Django project. We can
set them via the Meta class on our database models.

---

[190]https://docs.djangoproject.com/en/3.1/topics/auth/customizing/#custom-permissions

For example, let's add a special status so that an author can read all books. In other words they have access to the `DetailView`. We could be much more specific with the permissions, restricting them per book, but this is a good first step.

In the `books/models.py` file we'll add a `Meta` class and set both the permission name and a description which will be visible in the admin.

Code

```
# books/models.py
...
class Book(models.Model):
    id = models.UUIDField(
        primary_key=True,
        default=uuid.uuid4,
        editable=False)
    title = models.CharField(max_length=200)
    author = models.CharField(max_length=200)
    price = models.DecimalField(max_digits=6, decimal_places=2)
    cover = models.ImageField(upload_to='covers/', blank=True)

    class Meta: # new
        permissions = [
            ('special_status', 'Can read all books'),
        ]

    def __str__(self):
        return self.title

    def get_absolute_url(self):
        return reverse('book_detail', args=[str(self.id)])
...
```

The order of the inner classes and methods here is deliberate. It follows the Model style[a] section from the Django documentation.

[a]https://docs.djangoproject.com/en/3.1/internals/contributing/writing-code/coding-style/#model-style

Since we have updated our database model we must create a new migrations file and then apply it.

Command Line

```
$ docker-compose exec web python manage.py makemigrations books
$ docker-compose exec web python manage.py migrate
```

User Permissions

Now we need to apply this custom permission to our new `special` user. Thanks to the admin this is not a difficult task. Navigate to the `Users` section where the three existing users are listed: `special@email.com`, `testuser@email.com`, and `will@learndjango.com` which is my superuser account.

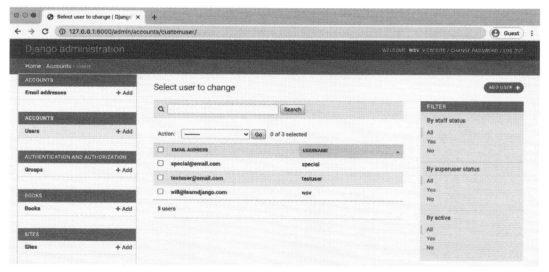

Three Users

Click on the `special@email.com` user and then scroll down to `User permissions` near the bottom of the page. Within it search for `books | book | Can read all books` and select it.

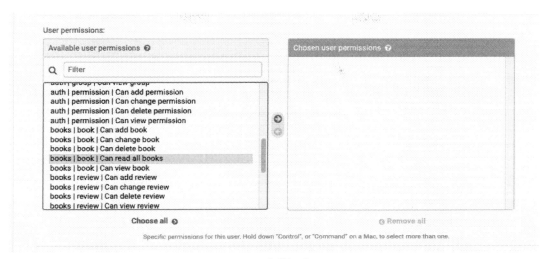

Can read all books

Click on the -> arrow to add it to "Chosen user permissions." Don't forget to click the "Save" button at the bottom of the page.

Add Permission

PermissionRequiredMixin

The last step is to apply the custom permission using the PermissionRequiredMixin[191]. One of the many great features of class-based views is we can implement advanced functionality with very little code on our part and this particular mixin is a good example of that.

Add PermissionRequiredMixin to our list of imports on the top line. Then add it to DetailView

---

[191]https://docs.djangoproject.com/en/3.1/topics/auth/default/#the-permissionrequiredmixin-mixin

after `LoginRequiredMixin` but before `DetailView`. The order should make sense: if a user isn't already logged in it makes no sense to do the additional check of whether they have permission. Finally add a `permission_required` field which specifies the desired permission. In our case its name is `special_status` and it exists on the `books` model.

Code

```
# books/views.py
from django.contrib.auth.mixins import (
    LoginRequiredMixin,
    PermissionRequiredMixin # new
)
from django.views.generic import ListView, DetailView
from .models import Book


class BookListView(LoginRequiredMixin, ListView):
    model = Book
    context_object_name = 'book_list'
    template_name = 'books/book_list.html'
    login_url = 'account_login'


class BookDetailView(
        LoginRequiredMixin,
        PermissionRequiredMixin, # new
        DetailView):
    model = Book
    context_object_name = 'book'
    template_name = 'books/book_detail.html'
    login_url = 'account_login'
    permission_required = 'books.special_status' # new
```

It is possible to add multiple permissions[192] via the `permission_required` field, though we are not doing so here.

To try out our work, log out of the admin. This is necessary because the superuser account is used for the admin and by default has access to everything. Not a great user account to test with!

Log in to the Bookstore site using the `testuser@email.com` account and then navigate to the Books page listing the three available titles. If you then click on any one of the books, you'll see

---

[192]https://docs.djangoproject.com/en/3.1/topics/auth/default/#the-permissionrequiredmixin-mixin

a "403 Forbidden" error because permission was denied.

403 Error Page

Now go back to the homepage at `http://127.0.0.1:8000/` and log out. Then log in using the `special@email.com` account. Navigate again to the Books page and each individual book page is accessible.

Groups & UserPassesTestMixin

The third permissions mixin available is UserPassesTestMixin[193] which restricts a view's access only to users who pass a specific test.

And in large projects Groups[194], which are Django's way of applying permissions to a category of users, become prominent. If you look on the Admin homepage there is a dedicated `Groups` section where they can be added and have permissions set. This is far more efficient than adding permissions on a per-user basis.

An example of groups is if you have a premium section on your website, a user upgrading could switch them into the premium group and then have access to however many specific extra permissions that involves.

Tests

It's a good idea to run tests whenever a code change has been made. After all, the whole point of testing is to check that we did not inadvertently cause another part of the application to fail.

---

[193]https://docs.djangoproject.com/en/3.1/topics/auth/default/#django.contrib.auth.mixins.
UserPassesTestMixin
[194]https://docs.djangoproject.com/en/3.1/topics/auth/default/#groups

Command Line

```
$ docker-compose exec web python manage.py test
...
Ran 17 tests in 0.519s

FAILED (failures=2)
```

It turns out we do have some failing tests! Specifically, `test_book_list_view` and `test_book_-detail_view` both complain of a `302` status code, meaning a redirection, rather than a `200` for success. This is because we've just added the requirement that log in is required to view the list of books and for a detail page the user must have a `special_status` permission.

The first step is to import `Permission` from the built-in auth models. Then within our `BookTests` in `books/tests.py` add the `special_status` permission to the `setUp` method so it is available for all our tests. We'll transfer the existing single `test_book_list_view` test into one for logged in users and one for logged out users. And we'll update the detail view test to check if a user has the correct permission.

Code

```python
# books/tests.py
from django.contrib.auth import get_user_model
from django.contrib.auth.models import Permission # new
from django.test import Client, TestCase
from django.urls import reverse

from .models import Book, Review


class BookTests(TestCase):

    def setUp(self):
        self.user = get_user_model().objects.create_user(
            username='reviewuser',
            email='reviewuser@email.com',
            password='testpass123'
        )
        self.special_permission = Permission.objects.get(
            codename='special_status') # new
        self.book = Book.objects.create(
            title='Harry Potter',
            author='JK Rowling',
```

```python
            price='25.00',
        )
        self.review = Review.objects.create(
            book = self.book,
            author = self.user,
            review = 'An excellent review',
        )

    def test_book_listing(self):
        ...

    def test_book_list_view_for_logged_in_user(self): # new
        self.client.login(email='reviewuser@email.com', password='testpass123')
        response = self.client.get(reverse('book_list'))
        self.assertEqual(response.status_code, 200)
        self.assertContains(response, 'Harry Potter')
        self.assertTemplateUsed(response, 'books/book_list.html')

    def test_book_list_view_for_logged_out_user(self):  # new
        self.client.logout()
        response = self.client.get(reverse('book_list'))
        self.assertEqual(response.status_code, 302)
        self.assertRedirects(
            response, '%s?next=/books/' % (reverse('account_login')))
        response = self.client.get(
            '%s?next=/books/' % (reverse('account_login')))
        self.assertContains(response, 'Log In')

    def test_book_detail_view_with_permissions(self): # new
        self.client.login(email='reviewuser@email.com', password='testpass123')
        self.user.user_permissions.add(self.special_permission)
        response = self.client.get(self.book.get_absolute_url())
        no_response = self.client.get('/books/12345/')
        self.assertEqual(response.status_code, 200)
        self.assertEqual(no_response.status_code, 404)
        self.assertContains(response, 'Harry Potter')
        self.assertContains(response, 'An excellent review')
        self.assertTemplateUsed(response, 'books/book_detail.html')
```

If you run the test suite again all tests should pass.

Command Line

```
$ docker-compose exec web python manage.py test
...
Ran 18 tests in 0.944s

OK
```

Git

Make sure to create a new Git commit for the changes in this chapter.

Command Line

```
$ git status
$ git add .
$ git commit -m 'ch13'
```

As always you can compare your code again the official source code on Github[195].

Conclusion

Permissions and groups are a highly subjective area that vary widely from project to project. However the basics remain the same and mimic what we've covered here. The first pass is typically to restrict access to only logged in users, then add additional custom permissions from there around groups or users.

In the next chapter we'll add search functionality to our Bookstore site.

---

[195]https://github.com/wsvincent/djangoforprofessionals/tree/master/ch13-permissions

Chapter 14: Search

Search is a fundamental feature of most websites and certainly anything e-commerce related like our Bookstore. In this chapter we will learn how to implement basic search with forms and filters. Then we will improve it with additional logic and touch upon ways to go even more deeply with search options in Django. We only have three books in our database now but the code here will scale to as many books as we'd like.

Search functionality consists of two parts: a form to pass along a user search query and then a results page that performs a filter based on that query. Determining "the right" type of filter is where search becomes interesting and hard. But first we need to create both a form and the search results page.

We could start with either one at this point, but we'll configure the filtering first and then the form.

Search Results Page

We'll start with the search results page. As with all Django pages that means adding a dedicated URL, view, and template. The implementation order doesn't particularly matter, but we will add them in that order.

Within `books/urls.py`, add a `search/` path with that URL name of `search_results` that uses a view called `SearchResultsListView`.

Code

```
# books/urls.py
from django.urls import path
from .views import BookListView, BookDetailView, SearchResultsListView # new

urlpatterns = [
    path('', BookListView.as_view(), name='book_list'),
    path('<uuid:pk>', BookDetailView.as_view(), name='book_detail'),
    path('search/', SearchResultsListView.as_view(),
        name='search_results'), # new
]
```

Next up is the view `SearchResultsListView` which is, for now, a listing of all available books. That's a prime candidate for using `ListView`. Its template will be called `search_results.html` and live within the `templates/books/` directory. The only new code is for `SearchResultsListView` as we have previously imported both `ListView` and the `Book` model at the top of the file.

Code

```
# books/views.py
...
class SearchResultsListView(ListView): # new
    model = Book
    context_object_name = 'book_list'
    template_name = 'books/search_results.html'
```

Last up is our template, `search_results.html`, which must be created.

Command Line

```
$ touch templates/books/search_results.html
```

For now it will list all available book's by title, author, and price.

Code

```
<!-- templates/books/search_results.html -->
{% extends '_base.html' %}

{% block title %}Search{% endblock title %}

{% block content %}
  <h1>Search Results</h1>
  {% for book in book_list %}
    <div>
      <h3><a href="{{ book.get_absolute_url }}">{{ book.title }}</a></h3>
      <p>Author: {{ book.author }}</p>
      <p>Price: $ {{ book.price }}</p>
    </div>
  {% endfor %}
{% endblock content %}
```

If you are still logged into a user account, log out now. The search results page is now available at `http://127.0.0.1:8000/books/search/`.

Search page

And there it is!

Basic Filtering

In Django a QuerySet[196] is used to filter the results from a database model. Currently our search results page doesn't feel like one because it is outputting *all* results from the Book model. Ultimately we want to run the filter based on the user's search query, but first we'll work through multiple filtering options.

It turns out there are multiple ways to customize a queryset including via a manager[197] on the model itself but to keep things simple, we can add a filter with just one line. So let's do that!

We can override the default queryset attribute on ListView which by default shows all results. The queryset documentation is quite robust and detailed, but often using contains[198] (which is case sensitive) or icontains[199] (which is not case sensitive) are good starting points. We will implement the filter based on the title that "contains" the name "beginners".

Code

```
# books/views.py
class SearchResultsListView(ListView):
    model = Book
    context_object_name = 'book_list'
    template_name = 'books/search_results.html'
    queryset = Book.objects.filter(title__icontains='beginners') # new
```

Refresh the search results page and now only a book with the title containing "beginners" is displayed. Success!

---

[196]https://docs.djangoproject.com/en/3.1/topics/db/queries/#retrieving-objects
[197]https://docs.djangoproject.com/en/3.1/topics/db/managers/#django.db.models.Manager
[198]https://docs.djangoproject.com/en/3.1/ref/models/querysets/#contains
[199]https://docs.djangoproject.com/en/3.1/ref/models/querysets/#icontains

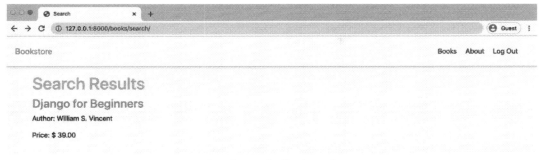

For basic filtering most of the time the built-in queryset methods[200] of `filter()`, `all()`, `get()`, or `exclude()` will be enough. However there is also a very robust and detailed QuerySet API[201] available as well that is worthy of further study.

Q Objects

Using `filter()` is powerful and it's even possible to chain filters[202] together such as search for all titles that contain "beginners" and "django". However often you'll want more complex lookups that can use "OR" not just "AND"; that's when it is time to turn to Q objects[203].

Here's an example where we set the filter to look for a result that matches a title of either "beginners" or "api". It's as simple as importing Q at the top of the file and then subtly tweaking our existing query. The | symbol represents the "or" operator. We can filter on any available field: not just `title` but also `author` or `price` as desired.

As the number of filters grows it can be helpful to separate out the `queryset` override via `get_-queryset()`. That's what we'll do here but note that this choice is optional.

---

[200] https://docs.djangoproject.com/en/3.1/topics/db/queries/#other-queryset-methods

[201] https://docs.djangoproject.com/en/3.1/ref/models/querysets/#queryset-api

[202] https://docs.djangoproject.com/en/3.1/topics/db/queries/#chaining-filters

[203] https://docs.djangoproject.com/en/3.1/topics/db/queries/#complex-lookups-with-q-objects

Code

```python
# books/views.py
from django.db.models import Q # new
...

class SearchResultsListView(ListView):
    model = Book
    context_object_name = 'book_list'
    template_name = 'books/book_list.html'

    def get_queryset(self): # new
        return Book.objects.filter(
            Q(title__icontains='beginners') | Q(title__icontains='api')
        )
```

Refresh the search results page to see the new result.

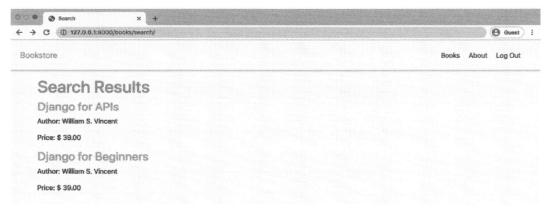

Search with Q objects

Now let's turn our attention to the corresponding search form so that rather than hardcode our filters in we can populate them based on the user's search query.

Forms

Fundamentally a web form is simple: it takes user input and sends it to a URL via either a GET or POST method. However in practice this fundamental behavior of the web can be monstrously complex.

The first issue is sending the form data: where does the data actually go and how do we handle it once there? Not to mention there are numerous security concerns whenever we allow users to submit data to a website.

There are only two options for "how" a form is sent: either via GET or POST HTTP methods.

A POST bundles up form data, encodes it for transmission, sends it to the server, and then receives a response. Any request that changes the state of the database–creates, edits, or deletes data–should use a POST.

A GET bundles form data into a string that is added to the destination URL. GET should only be used for requests that do not affect the state of the application, such as a search where nothing within the database is changing, basically we're just doing a filtered list view.

If you look at the URL after visiting Google.com you'll see your search query in the actual search results page URL itself.

For more information, Mozilla has detailed guides on both sending form data[204] and form data validation[205] that are worth reviewing if you're not already familiar with form basics.

Search Form

Let's add a basic search form to the current homepage right now. It can easily be placed in the navbar or on a dedicated search page as desired in the future.

We start with HTML `<form>` tags and use Bootstrap's styling to make them look nice. The `action` specifies where to redirect the user after the form is submitted, which will be the `search_results` page. As with all URL links this is the URL name for the page. Then we indicate the desired `method` of `get` rather than `post`.

The second part of the form is the `input` which contains the user search query. We provide it with a variable `name`, `q`, which will be later visible in the URL and also available in the views file. We add Bootstrap styling with the `class`, specify the `type` of input is text, add a `Placeholder` which is default text that prompts the user. The last part, `aria-label`, is the name provided to screen

---

[204]https://developer.mozilla.org/en-US/docs/Learn/HTML/Forms/Sending_and_retrieving_form_data
[205]https://developer.mozilla.org/en-US/docs/Learn/HTML/Forms/Form_validation

reader users. Accessibility is a big part of web development and should always be considered from the beginning: include `aria-labels` with all your forms!

Code

```
<!-- templates/home.html -->
{% extends '_base.html' %}
{% load static %}

{% block title %}Home{% endblock title %}

{% block content %}
  <h1>Homepage</h1>
  <form class="form-inline mt-2 mt-md-0" action="{% url 'search_results' %}"
  method="get">
    <input name="q" class="form-control mr-sm-2" type="text" placeholder="Search"
    aria-label="Search">
  </form>
{% endblock content %}
```

Navigate to the homepage and the new search box is present.

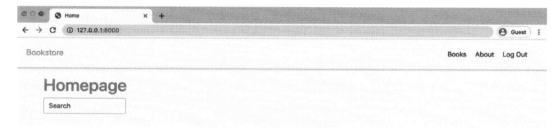

Homepage with search box

Try inputting a search, for example for "hello." Upon hitting Return you are redirected to the search results page. Note, in particular, the URL contains the search query `/search/?q=hello`.

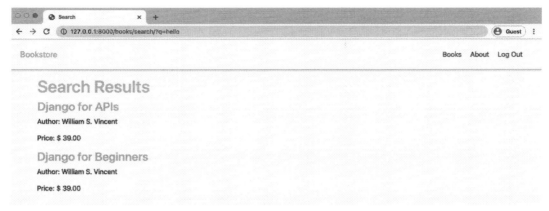

URL with query string

However the results haven't changed! And that's because our `SearchResultsListView` still has the hardcoded values from before. The last step is to take the user's search query, represented by q in the URL, and pass it in to the actual search filters.

Code

```python
# books/views.py
class SearchResultsListView(ListView):
    model = Book
    context_object_name = 'book_list'
    template_name = 'books/search_results.html'

    def get_queryset(self): # new
        query = self.request.GET.get('q')
        return Book.objects.filter(
            Q(title__icontains=query) | Q(author__icontains=query)
        )
```

What changed? We added a `query` variable that takes the value of q from the form submission. Then updated our filter to use `query` on either a `title` or an `author` field. That's it! Refresh the search results page–it still has the same URL with our query–and the result is expected: no results on either title or author for "hello".

Go back to the homepage and try a new search such as for "api" or "beginners" to see the complete search functionality in action.

Git

Make sure to save our current work in this chapter by committing the new code to Git.

Command Line

```
$ git status
$ git add .
$ git commit -m 'ch14'
```

The official source code for this chapter is available on Github[206].

Conclusion

Our basic search is now complete, but we've only scratched the surface of potential search optimizations. For example, maybe we want a button added to the search form that could be clicked in addition to hitting the Return key? Or better yet include form validation. Beyond filtering with ANDs and ORs there are other factors if we want a Google-quality search, things like relevancy and much more.

There are several third-party packages with enhanced features such as django-watson[207] or django-haystack[208] however, given that we're using PostgreSQL as the database, we can take advantage of its full text search[209] and other features which are built into Django itself.

A final option is either use an enterprise-level solution like ElasticSearch[210] that must be running on a separate server (not the hardest thing with Docker), or rely on a hosted solution like Swiftype[211] or Algolia[212].

In the next chapter we'll explore the many performance optimizations available in Django as we prepare our Bookstore project for eventual deployment.

---

[206]https://github.com/wsvincent/djangoforprofessionals/tree/master/ch14-search

[207]https://github.com/etianen/django-watson

[208]https://github.com/django-haystack/django-haystack

[209]https://docs.djangoproject.com/en/3.1/ref/contrib/postgres/search/

[210]https://www.elastic.co/

[211]https://swiftype.com/

[212]https://www.algolia.com/

Chapter 15: Performance

The first priority for any website is that it must work properly and contain proper tests. But if your project is fortunate enough to receive a large amount of traffic the focus quickly shifts to performance and making things as efficient as possible. This is a fun and challenging exercise for many engineers, but it can also be a trap.

The computer scientist Donald Knuth has a famous quote[213] worth reading in its entirety:

"The real problem is that programmers have spent far too much time worrying about efficiency in the wrong places and at the wrong times; premature optimization is the root of all evil (or at least most of it) in programming."

While it's important to set up proper monitoring so you *can* optimize your project later on, don't focus too much on it upfront. There's no way to properly mimic production environments locally. And there is no way to predict exactly how a site's traffic will look. But it is possible to spend far too much time seeking out tiny performance gains in the early stages instead of talking to users and making larger code improvements!

In this chapter we'll focus on the broad strokes of Django-related performance and highlight areas worth further investigation at scale. Generally speaking performance comes down to four major areas: optimizing database queries, caching, indexes, and compressing front-end assets like images, JavaScript, and CSS.

django-debug-toolbar

Before we can optimize our database queries we need to see them. And for this the default tool in the Django community is the third-party package django-debug-toolbar[214]. It comes with a configurable set of panels to inspect the complete request/response cycle of any given page.

Per usual we can install it within Docker and stop our running containers.

---

[213] http://www.paulgraham.com/knuth.html
[214] https://github.com/jazzband/django-debug-toolbar

Command Line

```
$ docker-compose exec web pipenv install django-debug-toolbar==2.2
$ docker-compose down
```

There are three separate configurations to set in our `config/settings.py` file:

1. `INSTALLED_APPS`
2. Middleware
3. `INTERNAL_IPS`

First add Debug Toolbar to the `INSTALLED_APPS` configuration. Note that the proper name is `debug_toolbar` not `django_debug_toolbar` as might be expected.

Code

```
# config/settings.py
INSTALLED_APPS = [
    'django.contrib.admin',
    'django.contrib.auth',
    'django.contrib.contenttypes',
    'django.contrib.sessions',
    'django.contrib.messages',
    'django.contrib.staticfiles',
    'django.contrib.sites',

    # Third-party
    'crispy_forms',
    'allauth',
    'allauth.account',
    'debug_toolbar', # new

    # Local
    'accounts',
    'pages',
    'books',
]
```

Second, add Debug Toolbar to the Middleware where it is primarily implemented.

Code

```
# config/settings.py
MIDDLEWARE = [
    'django.middleware.security.SecurityMiddleware',
    'django.contrib.sessions.middleware.SessionMiddleware',
    'django.middleware.common.CommonMiddleware',
    'django.middleware.csrf.CsrfViewMiddleware',
    'django.contrib.auth.middleware.AuthenticationMiddleware',
    'django.contrib.messages.middleware.MessageMiddleware',
    'django.middleware.clickjacking.XFrameOptionsMiddleware',
    'debug_toolbar.middleware.DebugToolbarMiddleware', # new
]
```

And third, set the INTERNAL_IPS[215] as well. If we were not in Docker this could be set to
'127.0.0.1', however, since we're running our web server within Docker an additional step is
required so that it matches the machine address of Docker. Add the following lines at the bottom
of config/settings.py.

Code

```
# config/settings.py
...
# django-debug-toolbar
import socket
hostname, _, ips = socket.gethostbyname_ex(socket.gethostname())
INTERNAL_IPS = [ip[:-1] + "1" for ip in ips]
```

Phew. That looks a bit scary, but basically it ensures that our INTERNAL_IPS matches that of our
Docker host.

Now rebuild the base image so it contains the package and the updated settings configuration.

Command Line

```
$ docker-compose up -d --build
```

There's one last step and that is to update our URLconf. We only want Debug Toolbar to appear if
DEBUG is true so we'll add logic to display it only in this case at the bottom of the config/urls.py
file.

---

[215]https://docs.djangoproject.com/en/3.1/ref/settings/#internal-ips

Code

```python
# config/urls.py
from django.conf import settings
from django.conf.urls.static import static
from django.contrib import admin
from django.urls import path, include

urlpatterns = [
    # Django admin
    path('admin/', admin.site.urls),

    # User management
    path('accounts/', include('allauth.urls')),

    # Local apps
    path('', include('pages.urls')),
    path('books/', include('books.urls')),
] + static(settings.MEDIA_URL, document_root=settings.MEDIA_ROOT)

if settings.DEBUG: # new
    import debug_toolbar
    urlpatterns = [
        path('__debug__/', include(debug_toolbar.urls)),
    ] + urlpatterns
```

Now if you refresh the homepage you'll see the `django-debug-toolbar` on the righthand side.

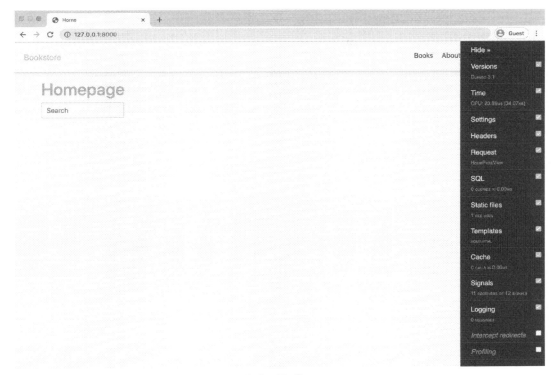

Debug Toolbar

If you click the "Hide" link on top it becomes a much smaller sidebar on the righthand side of the page.

Analyzing Pages

Debug Toolbar has many possible customizations[216] but the default settings visible tell us a lot about our homepage. For instance, we can see the current version of Django being used as well as the Time it took to load the page. Also the specific request called which was HomePageView. This may seem obvious but on large codebases especially if you are jumping in as a new developer, it may not be obvious which view is calling which page. Debug Toolbar is a helpful quickstart to understanding existing sites.

---

[216]https://django-debug-toolbar.readthedocs.io/en/latest/index.html

Probably the most useful item, however, is SQL which shows queries on a specific page. If you are logged out right now, there are no SQL queries on the homepage. So go ahead and log in with your superuser account and then return the homepage. Debug Toolbar shows that two queries are being run and the time of each.

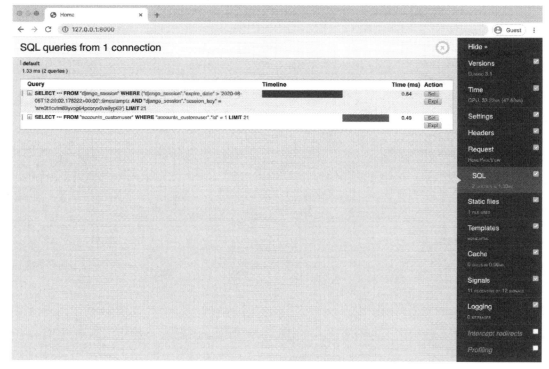

Debug Toolbar

Large and poorly optimized sites can have hundreds or even thousands of queries being run on a single page!

select_related and prefetch_related

What are the options if you do find yourself working on a Django site with way too many SQL queries per page? In general, though, fewer large queries will be faster than many smaller queries, though it's possible and required to test this in practice. Two common techniques for doing so are select_related()[217] and prefetch_related()[218].

`select_related` is used for single-value relationships through a forward one-to-many or a one-to-one relationship. It creates a SQL join and includes the fields of the related object in the `SELECT` statement, which results in all related objects being included in a single more complex database query. This single query is typically more performant than multiple, smaller queries.

`prefetch_related` is used for a set or list of objects like a many-to-many or many-to-one relationship. Under the hood a lookup is done for each relationship and the "join" occurs in Python, not SQL. This allows it to prefetch many-to-many and many-to-one objects, which cannot be done using select_related, in addition to the foreign key and one-to-one relationships that are supported by select_related.

Implementing one or both on a website is a common first pass towards reducing queries and loading time for a given page.

Caching

Consider that our Bookstore project is a dynamic website. Each time a user requests a page our server has to make various calculations including database queries, template rendering, and so on before servicing it. This takes time and is much slower than simply reading a file from a static site where the content does not change.

On large sites, though, this type of overhead can be quite slow and caching is one of the first solutions in a web developer's tool bag. Implementing caching on our current project is definitely overkill, but we will nonetheless review the options and implement a basic version.

A cache is an in-memory storing of an expensive calculation. Once executed it doesn't need to be run again! The two most popular options are Memcached[219] which features native Django support and Redis[220] which is commonly implemented with the django-redis[221] third-party package.

---

[217] https://docs.djangoproject.com/en/3.1/ref/models/querysets/#select-related
[218] https://docs.djangoproject.com/en/3.1/ref/models/querysets/#prefetch-related
[219] https://docs.djangoproject.com/en/3.1/topics/cache/#memcached
[220] https://redis.io/
[221] https://github.com/niwinz/django-redis

Django has its own cache framework[222] which includes four different caching options in descending order of granularity:

1) The per-site cache[223] is the simplest to set up and caches your entire site.

2) The per-view cache[224] lets you cache individual views.

3) Template fragment caching[225] lets you specify a specific section of a template to cache.

4) The low-level cache API[226] lets you manually set, retrieve, and maintain specific objects in the cache.

Why not just cache everything all the time? One reason is that cache memory is expensive, as it's stored as RAM: think about the cost of going from 8GB to 16GB of RAM on your laptop vs. 256GB to 512GB of hard drive space. Another is the cache must be "warm," that is filled with updated content, so depending upon the needs of a site, optimizing the cache so it is accurate, but not wasteful, takes quite a bit of tuning.

If you wanted to implement per-site caching, which is the simplest approach, you'd add `UpdateCacheMiddleware` at the very top of the `MIDDLEWARE` configuration in `config/settings.py` and `FetchFromCacheMiddleware` at the very bottom. Also set three additional fields CACHE_-MIDDLEWARE_ALIAS[227], CACHE_MIDDLEWARE_SECONDS[228], and CACHE_MIDDLEWARE_-KEY_PREFIX[229].

---

[222]https://docs.djangoproject.com/en/3.1/topics/cache/

[223]https://docs.djangoproject.com/en/3.1/topics/cache/#the-per-site-cache

[224]https://docs.djangoproject.com/en/3.1/topics/cache/#the-per-view-cache

[225]https://docs.djangoproject.com/en/3.1/topics/cache/#template-fragment-caching

[226]https://docs.djangoproject.com/en/3.1/topics/cache/#the-low-level-cache-api

[227]https://docs.djangoproject.com/en/3.1/ref/settings/#std:setting-CACHE_MIDDLEWARE_ALIAS

[228]https://docs.djangoproject.com/en/3.1/ref/settings/#cache-middleware-seconds

[229]https://docs.djangoproject.com/en/3.1/ref/settings/#cache-middleware-key-prefix

Code

```python
# config/settings.py
MIDDLEWARE = [
    'django.middleware.cache.UpdateCacheMiddleware', # new
    'django.middleware.security.SecurityMiddleware',
    'django.contrib.sessions.middleware.SessionMiddleware',
    'django.middleware.common.CommonMiddleware',
    'debug_toolbar.middleware.DebugToolbarMiddleware',
    'django.middleware.csrf.CsrfViewMiddleware',
    'django.contrib.auth.middleware.AuthenticationMiddleware',
    'django.contrib.messages.middleware.MessageMiddleware',
    'django.middleware.clickjacking.XFrameOptionsMiddleware',
    'debug_toolbar.middleware.DebugToolbarMiddleware',
    'django.middleware.cache.FetchFromCacheMiddleware', # new
]

CACHE_MIDDLEWARE_ALIAS = 'default'
CACHE_MIDDLEWARE_SECONDS = 604800
CACHE_MIDDLEWARE_KEY_PREFIX = ''
```

The only default you might want to adjust is CACHE_MIDDLEWARE_SECONDS which is the default number of seconds (600) to cache a page. After the period is up, the cache expires and becomes empty. A good default when starting out is 604800 seconds or 1 week (60secs x 60minutes x 168hours) for a site with content that doesn't change very often. But if you find your cache filling up rapidly or you are running a site where the content changes on a frequent basis, shortening this setting is a good first step.

Implementing caching is strictly optional at this point though. Once a website is up and running the need for caching–per site, per page, and so on–will quickly become apparent. There is also extra complexity as Memcache must be run as a separate instance. On the hosting service Heroku, which we'll use in chapter 18 for deployment, there is a free tier available via Memcachier[230].

Indexes

Indexing[231] is a common technique for speeding up database performance. It is a separate data

---

[230]https://elements.heroku.com/addons/memcachier

[231]https://en.wikipedia.org/wiki/Database_index

structure that allows faster searches and is typically only applied to the primary key in a model. The downside is that indexes require additional space on a disk so they must be used with care.

Tempting as it is to simply add indexes to primary keys from the beginning, it is better to start without them and only add them later based on production needs. A general rule of thumb is that if a given field is being used frequently, such as 10-25% of all queries, it is a prime candidate to be indexed.

Historically an index field could be created by adding `db_index=True` to any model field. For example, if we wanted to add one to the `id` field in our `Book` model it would look as follows (don't actually implement this though).

Code

```
# books/models.py
...
class Book(models.Model):
    id = models.UUIDField(
        primary_key=True,
        db_index=True, # new
        default=uuid.uuid4,
        editable=False)
...
```

This change would need to be added via a migration file and migrated.

Starting in Django 1.11[232], class-based model indexes were added so can include in the Meta section instead[233]. So you could write the previous index as follows instead:

[232]https://docs.djangoproject.com/en/3.1/releases/1.11/#class-based-model-indexes
[233]https://docs.djangoproject.com/en/3.1/ref/models/options/#indexes

Code

```
# books/models.py
...
class Book(models.Model):
    id = models.UUIDField(
        primary_key=True,
        default=uuid.uuid4,
        editable=False)
    ...

    class Meta:
        indexes = [ # new
            models.Index(fields=['id'], name='id_index'),
        ]
        permissions = [
            ("special_status", "Can read all books"),
        ]
```

Since we've changed the model we must create a migrations file and apply it.

Command Line

```
$ docker-compose exec web python manage.py makemigrations books
$ docker-compose exec web python manage.py migrate
```

django-extensions

Another very popular third-party package for inspecting a Django project is django-extensions[234] which adds a number of helpful custom extensions[235].

One that is particularly helpful is shell_plus[236] which will autoload all models into the `shell` which makes working with the Django ORM much easier.

---

[234]https://github.com/django-extensions/django-extensions
[235]https://django-extensions.readthedocs.io/en/latest/command_extensions.html
[236]https://django-extensions.readthedocs.io/en/latest/shell_plus.html

Front-end Assets

A final major source of bottlenecks in a website is loading front-end assets. CSS and JavaScript can become quite large and therefore tools like django-compressor[237] can help to minimize their size.

Images are often the first place to look in terms of asset size. The static/media file set up we have in place will scale to a quite large size, but for truly large sites it is worth investigating the use of a Content Delivery Network (CDN)[238] for images instead of storing them on the server filesystem.

You can also serve different size images to users. For example, rather than shrink down a large book cover for a list or search page you could store a smaller thumbnail version instead and serve *that* where needed. The third-party easy-thumbnails[239] package is a good place to start for this.

A fantastic free e-book on the topic is Essential Image Optimization[240] by Addy Osmani that goes into depth on image optimization and automations.

As a final check there are automated tests for front-end speed such as Google's PageSpeed Insights[241] that will assign a score based on how quickly a page loads.

Git

There's been a lot of code changes in this chapter so make sure to commit everything with Git.

---

[237] https://github.com/django-compressor/django-compressor
[238] https://en.wikipedia.org/wiki/Content_delivery_network
[239] https://github.com/SmileyChris/easy-thumbnails
[240] https://images.guide/
[241] https://developers.google.com/speed/pagespeed/insights/

Command Line

```
$ git status
$ git add .
$ git commit -m 'ch15'
```

If you have any errors make sure to look at your logs with `docker-compose logs` and compare your code with the official source code on Github[242].

Conclusion

There is an almost endless list of performance optimizations that can be applied to a project. But take care to recall Donald Knuth's sage advice and not go too crazy on this. Bottlenecks will reveal themselves in production and should largely be addressed then; not in advance.

You should remember that performance problems are a good problem to have! They are fixable and mean that your project is being heavily used.

---

[242]https://github.com/wsvincent/djangoforprofessionals/tree/master/ch15-performance

Chapter 16: Security

The World Wide Web is a dangerous place. There are many bad actors and even more auto-mated bots that *will* try to hack into your website and cause ill. Therefore understanding and implementing security features is a must in any website.

Fortunately, Django has a very strong record when it comes to security thanks to its years of experience handling web security issues as well as a robust and regular security update cycle. New feature releases[243] come out roughly every 9 months such as 2.2 to 3.0 but there are also patch releases around bugs and security like 2.2.2 to 2.2.3 that occur almost monthly.

However, as with any tool, it's important to implement security features correctly and in this chapter we'll cover how to do so in our Bookstore project.

Social Engineering

The biggest security risk to any website is ultimately not technical: it is people. The term social engineering[244] refers to the technique of finding individuals with access to a system who will willingly or unwillingly share their login credentials with a bad actor.

These days phishing[245] is probably the most likely culprit if you are in a technical organization. All it takes is one bad click on an email link for a malicious actor to potentially gain access to the system, or at least all the access the compromised employee has.

To mitigate this risk, implement a robust permissions scheme and only provide the exact security access an employee needs, not more. Does every engineer need access to the production database? Probably not. Do non-engineers need write access? Again, probably not. These are discussions best had up front and a good default is to only add permissions as needed, not to default to superuser status for everyone!

---

[243] https://www.djangoproject.com/download/
[244] https://en.wikipedia.org/wiki/Social_engineering_%28security%29
[245] https://en.wikipedia.org/wiki/Phishing

Django updates

Keeping your project up-to-date with the latest version of Django is another important way to stay secure. And I don't just mean being current with the latest feature release[246] (2.2, 3.0, 3.1, etc) which comes out roughly every 9 months. There are also monthly security patch updates that take the form of 2.2.1, 2.2.2, 2.2.3, etc.

What about **long-term support (LTS) releases**? Certain feature releases designated as LTS receive security and data loss fixes for a guaranteed period of time, usually around 3 years. For example, Django 2.2 is an LTS and will be supported into 2022 when Django 4.0 is released as the next LTS version. Can you stay on LTS versions? Yes. Should you? No. It is better and more secure to stay up-to-date.

Resist the temptation and reality of many real-world projects which is not to devote a portion of developer time to staying current with Django versions. A website is like a car: it needs regular maintenance to run at its best. You are only compounding the problem if you put off updates.

How to update? Django features deprecation warnings[247] that can and should be run for each new release by typing `python -Wa manage.py test`. It is far better to update from 2.0 to 2.1 to 2.2 and run the deprecation warnings each time rather than skipping multiple versions.

Deployment Checklist

To assist with with deployment and checking security settings, the Django docs contain a dedicated deployment checklist[248] that further describes security settings.

Even better there is a command we can run to automate Django's recommendations, `python manage.py check --deploy`, that will check if a project is deployment ready. It uses the Django system check framework[249] which can be used to customize similar commands in mature projects.

---

[246]https://www.djangoproject.com/download/
[247]https://docs.djangoproject.com/en/3.1/howto/upgrade-version/
[248]https://docs.djangoproject.com/en/3.1/howto/deployment/checklist/
[249]https://docs.djangoproject.com/en/3.1/topics/checks/

Since we are working in Docker we must prepend `docker-compose exec web` to the command though.

Command Line

```
$ docker-compose exec web python manage.py check --deploy
System check identified some issues:

WARNINGS:
...
System check identified 5 issues (0 silenced).
```

How nice! A descriptive and lengthy list of issues which we can go through one-by-one to prepare our Bookstore project for production.

docker-compose-prod.yml

Ultimately, our local development settings will differ from our production settings. We already started to configure this back in Chapter 8: Environment Variables. Recall that we added environment variables for SECRET_KEY, DEBUG, and DATABASES. But we did not set production values or a way to toggle efficiently between local and production.

There are a number of ways to tackle this challenge. Given we will be deploying on Heroku, our approach is to create a `docker-compose-prod.yml` file that we can use to test the production environment and we'll manually add environment variables to the production environment.

To start, create a `docker-compose-prod.yml` file in the same folder as `docker-compose.yml`.

Command Line

```
$ touch docker-compose-prod.yml
```

By default, Git will track every file or folder in our project. We *do not* want that to occur for this new file as it will contain sensitive information. The solution is to also create a file called `.gitignore`, which contains file or folders that will be ignored by Git.

Create the new file.

Command Line

```
$ touch .gitignore
```

Add our single file to it.

.gitignore

```
docker-compose-prod.yml
__pycache__/
db.sqlite3
.DS_Store # Mac only
```

If you're curious, Github maintains an official Python gitignore file[250] containing additional configurations worthy of further exploration.

Run `git status` again and the `docker-compose-prod.yml` file is not visible, even though it is still in our project. That's what we want!

For now, copy the `docker-compose.yml` file into `docker-compose-prod.yml`.

docker-compose-prod.yml

```
version: '3.8'

services:
  web:
    build: .
    command: python /code/manage.py runserver 0.0.0.0:8000
    volumes:
      - .:/code
    ports:
      - 8000:8000
    depends_on:
      - db
    environment:
      - "DJANGO_SECRET_KEY=)*_s#exg*#w+#-xt=vu8b010%%a&p@4edwyj0=(nqq90b9a8*n"
      - "DJANGO_DEBUG=True"
  db:
    image: postgres:11
    volumes:
      - postgres_data:/var/lib/postgresql/data/
```

---

[250]https://github.com/github/gitignore/blob/master/Python.gitignore

```
  environment:
    - "POSTGRES_HOST_AUTH_METHOD=trust"

volumes:
  postgres_data:
```

To run our new file, spin down the Docker host and restart it via the `-f` flag to specify an alternate compose file[251]. By default, Docker assumes a `docker-compose.yml` so adding the `-f` flag is unnecessary in that case.

Command Line

```
$ docker-compose down
$ docker-compose -f docker-compose-prod.yml up -d --build
$ docker-compose exec web python manage.py migrate
```

The `--build` flag is added for the initial building of the image, along with all the corresponding software packages, for the new compose file. Also `migrate` is run on the new database. This is an entirely new instance of our project! As such it won't have a superuser account or any of our data such as book information. But that's OK for now; that information can be added in production and our focus is on creating a local production testing environment.

Navigate to the website and everything should run as before, even though we are using a different compose file.

DEBUG

Ultimately, our goal in this chapter is to pass Django's deployment checklist by using the `docker-compose-prod.yml` file. Let's start by changing `DEBUG`, which is set to `True`, but should be `False` in production.

---

[251]https://docs.docker.com/compose/reference/overview/

docker-compose-prod.yml

```
environment:
  - "DJANGO_SECRET_KEY=)*_s#exg*#w+#-xt=vu8b010%%a&p@4edwyj0=(nqq90b9a8*n"
  - "DJANGO_DEBUG=False" # new
```

Spin down Docker and start it up again after making the change.

Command Line

```
$ docker-compose down
$ docker-compose -f docker-compose-prod.yml up -d --build
```

The website should run the same as before, but to check that DEBUG is set to False, visit a page that doesn't exist like http://127.0.0.1:8000/debug.

Debug Page Not Found

And there is a generic "Not Found" message, confirming we have DEBUG set to False. Because if it were True, there would be a detailed error report instead.

Let's run the Django deployment checklist again now that DEBUG has been changed. Recall that when we ran it earlier in the chapter there were 5 issues.

Command Line

```
$ docker-compose exec web python manage.py check --deploy
System check identified some issues:

WARNINGS:
...
System check identified 4 issues (0 silenced).
```

We're down to 4 since DEBUG is set to False. Progress!

Defaults

Environment variables serve two purposes in our Django project: they keep items like SECRET_KEY actually secret and they act as a way to toggle between local and production settings. While there is nothing wrong with having two environment variables for a setting like DEBUG, it is arguably cleaner to use a default value when we don't need to keep something secret.

For example, we could rewrite the DEBUG configuration to look as follows:

Code

```
# config/settings.py
DEBUG = env.bool("DJANGO_DEBUG", default=False)
```

This means default to a production value of False if no environment variable is present. If one is called DJANGO_DEBUG then use that. We would keep the DJANGO_DEBUG variable in the local docker-compose.yml file, but remove it in docker-compose-prod.yml. This approach results in a smaller docker-compose-prod.yml file and it is arguably more secure since if for some reason environment variables are not loading in properly, we won't turn on local development settings by accident. Only production values are used.

Go ahead and update docker-compose-prod.yml by removing DJANGO_DEBUG.

docker-compose-prod.yml

```
environment:
  - "DJANGO_SECRET_KEY=)*_s#exg*#w+#-xt=vu8b010%%a&p@4edwyj0=(nqq90b9a8*n"
```

If you spin down Docker and restart either the local or production settings both still work.

SECRET_KEY

Our SECRET_KEY is currently visible in the docker-compose.yml file. To be more secure, we should generate a new production key and test it via docker-compose-prod.yml. The SECRET_KEY is a 50-character random string generated anew each time the startproject command is run. To generate a new key we can use Python's built-in secrets[252] module.

Command Line

```
$ docker-compose exec web python -c 'import secrets; print(secrets.token_urlsafe(38))'
ldBHq0YGYxBzaMJnLVOiNG7hruE8WKzGG2zGpYxoTNmphB0mdBo
```

The parameter token_urlsafe returns the number of bytes in a URL-safe text string. With Base64 encoding on average each byte has 1.3 characters. So using 38 results in 51 characters in this case. The important thing is that your SECRET_KEY has at least 50 characters. Each time you run the command, a new value is outputted.

> A quick reminder that since we're working with Docker, if your SECRET_KEY includes a dollar
> sign, $, then you need to add an additional dollar sign, $$. This is due to how docker-compose
> handles variable substitution[a]. Otherwise you will see an error!
> _____
> [a]https://docs.docker.com/compose/compose-file/#variable-substitution

Add the new SECRET_KEY to the docker-compose-prod.yml file so it looks as follows:

_____
[252]https://docs.python.org/3/library/secrets.html

docker-compose-prod.yml

```
# docker-compose-prod.yml
environment:
  - "DJANGO_SECRET_KEY=ldBHq0YGYxBzaMJnLVOiNG7hruE8WKzGG2zGpYxoTNmphB0mdBo"
```

Restart our Docker container which now uses a truly secret SECRET_KEY.

Command Line

```
$ docker-compose down
$ docker-compose -f docker-compose-prod.yml up -d --build
```

The website should work just as before. There are four remaining issues to tackle in the deployment checklist but, first, a brief dive into web security so we can understand why these settings are important.

Web Security

Even though Django handles most common security issues by default, it is still vital to understand frequent attack methods and the steps Django takes to mitigate them. You can find an overview on the Django security page[253], but we'll go into further depth here.

Django comes by default with a number of additional security middlewares[254] that guard against other request/response cycle attacks.

A full explanation of each is beyond the scope of this book, but it is worth reading about the protections provided by the Django security team over the years. Do not change the defaults without good cause.

SQL injection

Let's start with a SQL injection attack[255] which occurs when a malicious user can execute arbitrary SQL code on a database. Consider a log in form on a site. What happens if a malicious

---

[253]https://docs.djangoproject.com/en/3.1/topics/security/

[254]https://docs.djangoproject.com/en/3.1/ref/middleware/#django.middleware.security.SecurityMiddleware

[255]https://en.wikipedia.org/wiki/SQL_injection

user instead types `DELETE from users WHERE user_id=user_id`? If this is run against the database without proper protections it could result in the deletion of all user records! Not good. This XKCD comic[256] provides a humorous though potentially accurate example of how this can occur.

Fortunately the Django ORM automatically sanitizes user inputs by default when constructing querysets to prevent this type of attack. Where you need to be careful is that Django does provide the option to execute custom sql[257] or raw queries[258]. These should both be used with extreme caution since they could open up a vulnerability to SQL injection.

The non-profit Open Web Application Security Project (OWASP) has a fantastic and very detailed SQL Injection Cheat Sheet[259] that is recommended for further reading.

XSS (Cross Site Scripting)

Cross-site scripting (XSS)[260] is another classic attack that occurs when an attacker is able to inject small bits of code onto web pages viewed by other people. This code, typically JavaScript, if stored in the database will then be retrieved and displayed to other users.

For example, consider the form used for writing book reviews on our current site. What if instead of typing, "This book was great" a user typed something with JavaScript? For example, `<script>alert('hello');</script>`. If this script were stored on the database then every future user's page would have a pop-up saying "hello". While this particular example is more annoying than dangerous, a site vulnerable to XSS is very dangerous because a malicious user could insert *any JavaScript* into the page, including JavaScript that steals pretty much anything from an unsuspecting user.

To prevent an XSS attack Django templates automatically escape[261] specific characters that are potentially dangerous including brackets (< and >), single quotes ', double quotes ", and the

---

[256]https://www.xkcd.com/327/

[257]https://docs.djangoproject.com/en/3.1/topics/db/sql/#executing-custom-sql

[258]https://docs.djangoproject.com/en/3.1/topics/db/sql/#executing-raw-queries

[259]https://github.com/OWASP/CheatSheetSeries/blob/master/cheatsheets/SQL_Injection_Prevention_
Cheat_Sheet.md

[260]https://en.wikipedia.org/wiki/Cross-site_scripting

[261]https://docs.djangoproject.com/en/3.1/ref/templates/language/#automatic-html-escaping

ampersand &. There are some edge cases where you might want to turn autoescape off[262] but this should be used with extreme caution.

OWASP's XSS Cheat Sheet[263] is recommended for further reading.

Cross-Site Request Forgery (CSRF)

A Cross-Site Request Forgery (CSRF)[264] is the third major type of attack but generally lesser known than SQL Injection or XSS. Fundamentally it exploits that trust a site has in a user's web browser.

When a user logs in to a website, let's call it a banking website for illustration purposes, the server sends back a session token for that user. This is included in the HTTP Headers of all future requests and authenticates the user. But what happens if a malicious actor somehow obtains access to this session token?

For example, consider a user who logs into their bank in one browser tab. Then in another tab they open their email and click on an email link from a malicious actor. This link looks legitimate, but in fact it is pointing to the user's bank which they are *still logged into*! So instead of leaving a blog comment on this fake site, behind the scenes the user's credentials are used to transfer money from their account to the hacker's account.

In practice there are multiple ways to obtain a user's credentials via a CSRF attack, not just links, but hidden forms, special image tags, and even AJAX requests.

Django provides CSRF protection[265] by including a random secret key both as a cookie via CSRF Middleware[266] and in a form via the csrf_token[267] template tag. A 3rd party website will not have access to a user's cookies and therefore any discrepancy between the two keys causes an error.

As ever, Django does allow customization: you can disable the CSRF middleware and use the

---

[262]https://docs.djangoproject.com/en/3.1/ref/templates/builtins/#std:templatetag-autoescape

[263]https://github.com/OWASP/CheatSheetSeries/blob/master/cheatsheets/Cross_Site_Scripting_
Prevention_Cheat_Sheet.md

[264]https://en.wikipedia.org/wiki/Cross-site_request_forgery

[265]https://docs.djangoproject.com/en/3.1/ref/csrf/#how-it-works

[266]https://docs.djangoproject.com/en/3.1/ref/middleware/#django.middleware.csrf.CsrfViewMiddleware

[267]https://docs.djangoproject.com/en/3.1/ref/templates/builtins/#csrf-token

csrf_protect()[268] template tag on specific views. However, undertake this step with extreme caution.

The OWASP CSRF Cheat Sheet[269] provides a comprehensive look at the issue. Almost all major websites have been victims of CSRF attacks at some point in time.

A good rule of thumb is whenever you have a form on your site, think about whether you need to include the `csrf_token` tag in it. Most of the time you will!

Clickjacking Protection

Clickjacking[270] is yet another attack where a malicious site tricks a user into clicking on a hidden frame. An internal frame, known as an iframe, is commonly used to embed one website within another. For example, if you wanted to include a Google Map or YouTube video on your site you would include the `iframe` tag that puts that site within your own. This is very convenient.

But it has a security risk which is that a frame can be hidden from a user. Consider if a user is already logged into their Amazon account and then visits a malicious site that purports to be a picture of kittens. The user clicks on said malicious site to see more kittens, but in fact they click an iFrame of an Amazon item that is unknowingly purchased. This is but one example of clickjacking.

To prevent against this Django comes with a default clickjacking middleware[271] that sets a X-Frame-Options HTTP header[272] that indicates whether a resource is allowed to load within a frame or iframe. You can turn this protection off, if desired, or even set it at a per view level. However, do so with a high degree of caution and research[273].

---

[268]https://docs.djangoproject.com/en/3.1/ref/csrf/#django.views.decorators.csrf.csrf_protect
[269]https://github.com/OWASP/CheatSheetSeries/blob/master/cheatsheets/Cross-Site_Request_Forgery_
Prevention_Cheat_Sheet.md
[270]https://en.wikipedia.org/wiki/Clickjacking
[271]https://docs.djangoproject.com/en/3.1/ref/clickjacking/#clickjacking-prevention
[272]https://developer.mozilla.org/en-US/docs/Web/HTTP/Headers/X-Frame-Options
[273]https://github.com/OWASP/CheatSheetSeries/blob/master/cheatsheets/Clickjacking_Defense_Cheat_
Sheet.md

HTTPS/SSL

All modern websites should use HTTPS[274], which provides encrypted communication between a client and server. HTTP (Hypertext Transfer Protocol)[275] is the backbone of the modern web, but it does not, by default, have encryption.

The "s" in HTTPS refers to its encrypted nature first due to SSL (Secure Sockets Layer) and these days its successor TLS (Transport Layer Security)[276]. With HTTPS enabled, which we will do in our deployment chapter, malicious actors can't sniff the incoming and outgoing traffic for data like authentication credentials or API keys.

One of the 4 remaining issues in our Django deployment checklist is that SECURE_SSL_REDIRECT is currently set to False. For security reasons, it's far better to force this to be True in production. Let's change that now by defaulting the configuration to True and adding the local development value to docker-compose.yml.

Code

```
# config/settings.py
SECURE_SSL_REDIRECT = env.bool("DJANGO_SECURE_SSL_REDIRECT", default=True)
```

Then add the environment variable to docker-compose.yml where it is set to False.

docker-compose.yml

```
# docker-compose.yml
environment:
  - "DJANGO_SECRET_KEY=)*_s#exg*#w+#-xt=vu8b010%%a&p@4edwyj0=(nqq90b9a8*n"
  - "DJANGO_DEBUG=True"
  - "DJANGO_SECURE_SSL_REDIRECT=False" # new
```

Restart Docker and run the deployment checklist again.

---

[274]https://en.wikipedia.org/wiki/HTTPS
[275]https://en.wikipedia.org/wiki/Hypertext_Transfer_Protocol
[276]https://en.wikipedia.org/wiki/Transport_Layer_Security

Command Line

```
$ docker-compose down
$ docker-compose -f docker-compose-prod.yml up -d --build
$ docker-compose exec web python manage.py check --deploy
```

We're down to 3 issues.

HTTP Strict Transport Security (HSTS)

HTTP Strict Transport Security (HSTS)[277] is a security policy that lets our server enforce that web browsers should only interact via HTTPS by adding a Strict-Transport-Security header[278].

There are three implicit HSTS configurations in our `settings.py` file that need to be updated for production:

- SECURE_HSTS_SECONDS[279] = 0
- SECURE_HSTS_INCLUDE_SUBDOMAINS[280] = False
- SECURE_HSTS_PRELOAD[281] = False

The `SECURE_HSTS_SECONDS` setting is set to 0 by default but the greater the better for security purposes. We will set it to one month, 2,592,000 seconds, in our project.

`SECURE_HSTS_INCLUDE_SUBDOMAINS` forces subdomains to also exclusively use SSL so we will set it to `True` in production.

`SECURE_HSTS_PRELOAD` only has an effect when there is a non-zero value for `SECURE_HSTS_-SECONDS`, but since we just set one, we'll need to set this to `True`.

Here is what the updated settings file should look like.

---

[277] https://en.wikipedia.org/wiki/HTTP_Strict_Transport_Security
[278] https://docs.djangoproject.com/en/3.1/ref/middleware/#http-strict-transport-security
[279] https://docs.djangoproject.com/en/3.1/ref/settings/#std:setting-SECURE_HSTS_SECONDS
[280] https://docs.djangoproject.com/en/3.1/ref/settings/#secure-hsts-include-subdomains
[281] https://docs.djangoproject.com/en/3.1/ref/settings/#secure-hsts-preload

Code

```
# config/settings.py
SECURE_HSTS_SECONDS = env.int("DJANGO_SECURE_HSTS_SECONDS", default=2592000)
SECURE_HSTS_INCLUDE_SUBDOMAINS = env.bool("DJANGO_SECURE_HSTS_INCLUDE_SUBDOMAINS",
    default=True)
SECURE_HSTS_PRELOAD = env.bool("DJANGO_SECURE_HSTS_PRELOAD", default=True)
```

Then update `docker-compose.yml` with the local development values.

docker-compose.yml

```
# docker-compose.yml
environment:
  - "DJANGO_SECRET_KEY=)*_s#exg*#w+#-xt=vu8b010%%a&p@4edwyj0=(nqq90b9a8*n"
  - "DJANGO_DEBUG=True"
  - "DJANGO_SECURE_SSL_REDIRECT=False"
  - "DJANGO_SECURE_HSTS_SECONDS=0" # new
  - "DJANGO_SECURE_HSTS_INCLUDE_SUBDOMAINS=False" # new
  - "DJANGO_SECURE_HSTS_PRELOAD=False" # new
```

Restart Docker and run the deployment checklist again.

Command Line

```
$ docker-compose down
$ docker-compose -f docker-compose-prod.yml up -d --build
$ docker-compose exec web python manage.py check --deploy
```

Only 2 issues left!

Secure Cookies

An HTTP Cookie[282] is used to store information on a client's computer such as authentication credentials. This is necessary because the HTTP protocol is stateless by design: there's no way to tell if a user is authenticated other than including an identifier in the HTTP Header!

---

[282]https://en.wikipedia.org/wiki/HTTP_cookie

Django uses sessions and cookies for this, as do most websites. But cookies can and should be forced over HTTPS as well via the SESSION_COOKIE_SECURE[283] config. Django's default setting is `False` so we must change it to `True` in production.

The second issue is CSRF_COOKIE_SECURE[284], which defaults to `False` but in production should be `True` so that only cookies marked as "secure" will be sent with an HTTPS connection.

Code

```
# config/settings.py
SESSION_COOKIE_SECURE = env.bool("DJANGO_SESSION_COOKIE_SECURE", default=True)
CSRF_COOKIE_SECURE = env.bool("DJANGO_CSRF_COOKIE_SECURE", default=True)
```

Then update the `docker-compose.yml` file.

docker-compose.yml

```
# docker-compose.yml
environment:
  - "DJANGO_SECRET_KEY=)*_s#exg*#w+#-xt=vu8b010%%a&p@4edwyj0=(nqq90b9a8*n"
  - "DJANGO_DEBUG=True"
  - "DJANGO_SECURE_SSL_REDIRECT=False"
  - "DJANGO_SECURE_HSTS_SECONDS=0"
  - "DJANGO_SECURE_HSTS_INCLUDE_SUBDOMAINS=False"
  - "DJANGO_SECURE_HSTS_PRELOAD=False"
  - "DJANGO_SESSION_COOKIE_SECURE=False" # new
  - "DJANGO_CSRF_COOKIE_SECURE=False" # new
```

Restart Docker and run the deployment checklist again.

---

[283]https://docs.djangoproject.com/en/3.1/ref/settings/#std:setting-SESSION_COOKIE_SECURE
[284]https://docs.djangoproject.com/en/3.1/ref/settings/#csrf-cookie-secure

Command Line

```
$ docker-compose down
$ docker-compose -f docker-compose-prod.yml up -d --build
$ docker-compose exec web python manage.py check --deploy
System check identified no issues (0 silenced).
```

No more issues. Woohoo!

Admin Hardening

So far it may seem as though the general security advice is to rely on Django defaults, use HTTPS, add `csrf_token` tags on forms, and set a permissions structure. All true. But one additional step Django does not take on our behalf is hardening the Django admin.

Consider that every Django website sets the admin, by default, to the /admin URL. This is a prime suspect for any hacker trying to access a Django site. Therefore, an easy step is to simply change the admin URL to literally anything else! Open up and change the URL path. In this example it is anything-but-admin/.

Code

```
# config/urls.py
from django.conf import settings
from django.conf.urls.static import static
from django.contrib import admin
from django.urls import path, include

urlpatterns = [
    # Django admin
    path('anything-but-admin/', admin.site.urls), # new

    # User management
    path('accounts/', include('allauth.urls')),

    # Local apps
    path('', include('pages.urls')),
    path('books/', include('books.urls')),
]

if settings.DEBUG:
```

```
import debug_toolbar
urlpatterns = [
    path('__debug__/', include(debug_toolbar.urls)),
] + urlpatterns
```

A fun 3rd party package django-admin-honeypot[285] will generate a fake admin log in screen and email site admins[286] the IP address of anyone trying to attack your site at /admin. These IP addresses can then be added to a blocked address list for the site.

It's also possible via django-two-factor-auth[287] to add two-factor authentication to your admin for an even further layer of protection.

Git

This chapter has been particularly heavy on code changes so make sure to commit all the updates with Git.

Command Line

```
$ git status
$ git add .
$ git commit -m 'ch16'
```

If you have any errors, check your logs with docker-compose logs and compare you code with the official source code on Github[288].

Conclusion

Security is a major concern for any website. By using a docker-compose-prod.yml file we can accurately test, within Docker, our production settings *before* deploying the site live. And by using default values we can both simplify the environment variables in the file as well as ensure

---

[285]https://github.com/dmpayton/django-admin-honeypot
[286]https://docs.djangoproject.com/en/3.1/ref/settings/#admins
[287]https://github.com/Bouke/django-two-factor-auth
[288]https://github.com/wsvincent/djangoforprofessionals/tree/master/ch16-security

that if something goes awry with environment variables we will default to production values, not unsecure local ones! Django comes with many built-in security features and with the addition of the deployment checklist we can now deploy our site now with a high degree of confidence that it is secure.

Ultimately, security is a constant battle and while the steps in this chapter cover most areas of concern, keeping your website up-to-date with the latest Django version is vital for continued safety.

Chapter 17: Deployment

So far we have been working entirely in a local development environment on our computer. But now it is time to deploy our project so that it is accessible to the public. In truth, the topic of deployment is worth an entire book on its own. Compared to other web frameworks Django is very hands-off and agnostic on the topic. There are no one-click deploys for most hosting platforms and while this requires more developer work it also allows, in typical Django fashion, for a high degree of customization.

In the previous chapter we configured a completely separate `docker-compose-prod.yml` file and updated `config/settings.py` to be production-ready. In this chapter we'll review how to choose a hosting provider, add a production-ready web server, and properly configure static/media files before deploying our Bookstore site!

PaaS vs IaaS

The first question is whether to use a Platform-as-a-Service (PaaS) or Infrastructure-as-a-Service (IaaS). A PaaS is an opinionated hosting option that handles much of the initial configuration and scaling needed for a website. Popular examples include Heroku[289], PythonAnywhere[290], and Dokku[291] among many others. While a PaaS costs more money upfront than an IaaS it saves an incredible amount of developer time, handles security updates automatically, and can be quickly scaled.

An IaaS by contrast provides total flexibility is typically cheaper, but it requires a high degree of knowledge and effort to properly set up. Prominent IaaS options include DigitalOcean[292],

---

[289]https://www.heroku.com/
[290]https://www.pythonanywhere.com/details/django_hosting
[291]http://dokku.viewdocs.io/dokku/
[292]https://www.digitalocean.com/

Linode[293], Amazon EC2[294], and Google Compute Engine[295] among many others.

So which one to use? Django developers tend to fall in one of two camps: either they already have a deployment pipeline configured with their IaaS of choice or they use a PaaS. Since the former is far more complex and varies widely in its configuration, we will use a PaaS in this book, specifically Heroku.

The choice of Heroku is somewhat arbitrary, but it is a mature technology that comes with a truly free tier sufficient for deploying our Bookstore project.

WhiteNoise

For local development Django relies on the staticfiles app[296] to automatically gather and serve static files from across the entire project. This is convenient, but quite inefficient and likely insecure, too.

For production the collectstatic[297] must be run to compile all static files into a single directory specified by STATIC_ROOT[298]. They can then be served either on the same server, a separate server, or a dedicated cloud service/CDN by updating STATICFILES_STORAGE[299].

In our project, we will rely on serving files from our server with the aid of the WhiteNoise[300] project which works extremely well on Heroku and is both faster and more configurable than Django defaults.

The first step is to install `whitenoise` within Docker and stop the running containers.

---

[293]https://www.linode.com/
[294]https://aws.amazon.com/ec2/
[295]https://cloud.google.com/compute/
[296]https://docs.djangoproject.com/en/3.1/ref/contrib/staticfiles/#module-django.contrib.staticfiles
[297]https://docs.djangoproject.com/en/3.1/ref/contrib/staticfiles/#collectstatic
[298]https://docs.djangoproject.com/en/3.1/ref/settings/#std:setting-STATIC_ROOT
[299]https://docs.djangoproject.com/en/3.1/ref/settings/#std:setting-STATICFILES_STORAGE
[300]https://github.com/evansd/whitenoise

Command Line

```
$ docker-compose exec web pipenv install whitenoise==5.1.0
$ docker-compose down
```

We won't rebuild the image just yet because we also have to make changes to our settings. Since we're using Docker it's possible to switch to WhiteNoise locally as well as in production. While it's possible to do this by passing in a --nostatic flag to the runserver command, this becomes tiring in practice. A better approach is to add whitenoise.runserver_nostatic before django.contrib.staticfiles in the INSTALLED_APPS config which will do the same thing. We'll also add it to our MIDDLEWARE right below SecurityMiddleware and update STATICFILES_STORAGE to use WhiteNoise now.

Code

```
# config/settings.py
INSTALLED_APPS = [
    'django.contrib.admin',
    'django.contrib.auth',
    'django.contrib.contenttypes',
    'django.contrib.sessions',
    'django.contrib.messages',
    'whitenoise.runserver_nostatic', # new
    'django.contrib.staticfiles',
    'django.contrib.sites',
    ...
]

MIDDLEWARE = [
  'django.middleware.cache.UpdateCacheMiddleware',
  'django.middleware.security.SecurityMiddleware',
  'whitenoise.middleware.WhiteNoiseMiddleware', # new
  ...
]

STATICFILES_STORAGE =
    'whitenoise.storage.CompressedManifestStaticFilesStorage' # new
```

With all our changes made we can now start up our project again in local development mode.

Command Line

```
$ docker-compose up -d --build
```

WhiteNoise has additional options to serve compressed content and far-future cache headers on content that won't change. But for now, go ahead and run the `collectstatic` command one more time.

Command Line

```
$ docker-compose exec web python manage.py collectstatic
```

There will be a warning about overwriting existing files. That's fine. Type "yes" and then hit the "Return" key to continue.

Media Files

WhiteNoise unfortunately does not work well with user-uploaded media files. Our book covers are added via the Django admin, but in a method similar to user-uploaded files. As a result, while they will appear as desired in local development, they will not show up in a production setting. See the docs for more information[301].

The recommended approach is to use the very popular django-storages[302] package alongside a dedicated CDN like S3. However this requires additional configuration that is beyond the scope of this book.

Gunicorn

When we ran the `startproject` command way back in Chapter 3 a `wsgi.py` file was created with a default WSGI (Web Server Gateway Interface)[303] configuration. This is a specification for how a web app (like our Bookstore project) communicates with a web server.

---

[301]http://whitenoise.evans.io/en/stable/django.html#serving-media-files
[302]https://django-storages.readthedocs.io/en/latest/
[303]https://wsgi.readthedocs.io/en/latest/

For production it is common to swap this out for either Gunicorn[304] or uWSGI[305]. Both offer a performance boost, but Gunicorn is more focused and simpler to implement so it will be our choice.

The first step is to install it within our project and stopping our containers.

Command Line

```
$ docker-compose exec web pipenv install gunicorn==20.0.4
$ docker-compose down
```

Because we are using Docker our local environment can mimic production quite easily so we'll update both docker-compose.yml and docker-compose-prod.yml to use Gunicorn instead of the local server.

docker-compose.yml

```
# command: python /code/manage.py runserver 0.0.0.0:8000
command: gunicorn config.wsgi -b 0.0.0.0:8000 # new
```

docker-compose-prod.yml

```
# command: python /code/manage.py runserver 0.0.0.0:8000
command: gunicorn config.wsgi -b 0.0.0.0:8000 # new
```

Now start up the containers again building a new image with the Gunicorn package and our updated environment variables.

Command Line

```
$ docker-compose up -d --build
```

---

[304]https://gunicorn.org/
[305]https://uwsgi-docs.readthedocs.io/en/latest/

Heroku

Head over to the Heroku[306] website and sign up for a free account. After you confirm your email Heroku will redirect you to the dashboard section of the site.

Next make sure to install Heroku's *Command Line Interface (CLI)* so we can deploy from the command line. There are detailed instructions here[307].

The final step is to log in with your Heroku credentials via the command line by typing `heroku login`. Use the email and password for Heroku you just set.

Command Line

```
$ heroku login
```

All set! If you have any issues you can type `heroku help` on the command line or visit the Heroku site for additional information.

Deploying with Docker

Now we are presented with a choice: deploy the traditional way on Heroku or with Docker containers. The latter is a new approach Heroku and other hosting providers have only recently added. However, just as Docker has taken over local development, it is starting to take over deployments as well. And once you've configured containers for deployment it is far easy to switch between potential hosting providers rather than if you configure their specific way. So we will deploy with Docker containers.

Even then we have, yet again, a choice to make as there are two different container options available[308]: using a container registry to deploy pre-built images or adding a `heroku.yml` file. We will use the latter approach as it will allow additional commands and more closely mimics the traditional Heroku approach of adding a `Procfile` for configuration.

---

[306]https://www.heroku.com/

[307]https://devcenter.heroku.com/articles/getting-started-with-python#set-up

[308]https://devcenter.heroku.com/categories/deploying-with-docker

heroku.yml

Traditional non-Docker Heroku relies on a custom `Procfile` for configuring a site for deployment. For containers Heroku relies on a similar approach of a custom file but called heroku.yml[309] in the root directory. It is similar to `docker-compose.yml` which is used for building local Docker containers.

Let's create our `heroku.yml` file now.

Command Line

```
$ touch heroku.yml
```

There are four top-level sections[310] available for configuration: `setup`, `build`, `release`, and `run`.

The main function of `setup` is to specify which add-ons are needed. These are hosted solutions Heroku provides, typically for a fee. The big one is our database which will rely on the free heroku-postgresql[311] tier. Heroku takes care of provisioning it, security updates, and we can easily upgrade the database size and uptime as needed.

The `build` section is how we specify the `Dockerfile` should be, well, built. This relies on our current `Dockerfile` in the root directory.

The `release` phase is used to run tasks before each new release is deployed. For example, we can make sure `collectstatic` is run on every deploy automatically.

Finally there is the `run` phase where we specify which processes actually run the application. Notably, the use of `Gunicorn` as the web server.

---

[309]https://devcenter.heroku.com/articles/build-docker-images-heroku-yml
[310]https://devcenter.heroku.com/articles/build-docker-images-heroku-yml#heroku-yml-overview
[311]https://elements.heroku.com/addons/heroku-postgresql

heroku.yml

```
setup:
  addons:
  - plan: heroku-postgresql
build:
  docker:
    web: Dockerfile
release:
  image: web
  command:
    - python manage.py collectstatic --noinput
run:
  web: gunicorn config.wsgi
```

Make sure to add the new deployment updates to Git and commit them. In the next section we'll push all our local code to Heroku itself.

Command Line

```
$ git status
$ git add .
$ git commit -m 'ch17'
```

Heroku Deployment

Now create a new app on Heroku for our Bookstore project. If you type `heroku create` Heroku will assign a random name. Since names are global in Heroku, it's unlikely that common ones like "blog" or "webapp" will be available. The name can always be changed later within Heroku to an available global namespace.

Command Line

```
$ heroku create
Creating app... done, â¬¢ fast-ravine-89805
https://fast-ravine-89805.herokuapp.com/ |
https://git.heroku.com/fast-ravine-89805.git
```

In this case Heroku assigned my app the name `fast-ravine-89805`. If you refresh the Heroku dashboard on the website you will now see the newly created app. Click on the new app to open the "Overview" page.

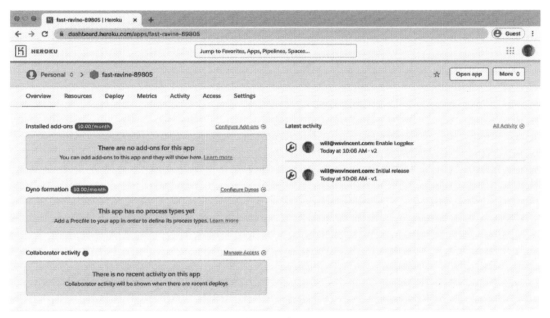

Heroku Overview Page

The next step is to add our production environment variables. Click on the "Settings" option at the top of the page and then click on "Reveal Config Vars." Because we are using defaults so liberally, there are only two values to set: the `DJANGO_SECRET_KEY` and `DJANGO_-ALLOWED_HOSTS`. And since we just discovered the specific domain name of our production site—`fast-ravine-89805.herokuapp.com/` in my case—we can add that to the `ALLOWED_HOSTS` now for maximum security.

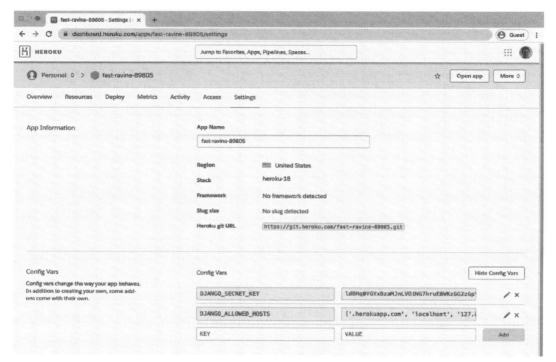

Heroku Config Vars

It's also possible to add config variables from the command line to Heroku. Both approaches work.

Now set the stack[312] to use our Docker containers, not Heroku's default buildpack. Include your app name here at the end of the command after `heroku stack:set container -a`.

Command Line

```
$ heroku stack:set container -a fast-ravine-89805
Setting stack to container... done
```

To confirm this change executed correctly, refresh the Heroku dashboard web page and note that under the "Info" section for "Stack" it now features "container." That's what we want.

---

[312]https://devcenter.heroku.com/articles/stack

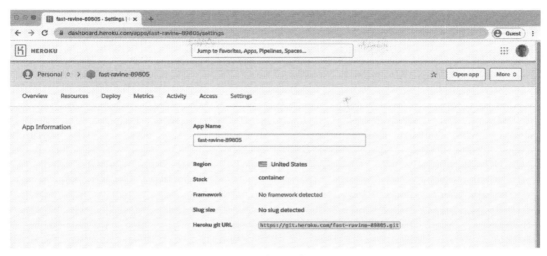

Heroku Stack

Before pushing our code to Heroku specify the hosted PostgreSQL database we want. In our case, the free `hobby-dev` tier works well; it can always be updated in the future.

Command Line

```
$ heroku addons:create heroku-postgresql:hobby-dev -a fast-ravine-89805
Creating heroku-postgresql:hobby-dev on â¬¢ fast-ravine-89805... free
Database has been created and is available
 ! This database is empty. If upgrading, you can transfer
 ! data from another database with pg:copy
Created postgresql-curved-34718 as DATABASE_URL
Use heroku addons:docs heroku-postgresql to view documentation
```

Did you notice how the DATABASE_URL variable was automatically created there. That's why we did not have to set it as a production environment variable.

We're ready! Create a Heroku remote[313], which means a version of our code that will live on a Heroku-hosted server. Make sure to include -a and the name of your app. Then "push" the code to Heroku which will result in building our Docker image and running the containers.

---

[313]https://devcenter.heroku.com/articles/git#creating-a-heroku-remote

Command Line

```
$ heroku git:remote -a fast-ravine-89805
set git remote heroku to https://git.heroku.com/fast-ravine-89805.git
$ git push heroku master
```

The initial push might take a while to complete. You can see active progress by clicking on the "Activity" tab on the Heroku dashboard.

Our Bookstore project should now be available online. Remember that while the code mirrors our own local code, the production site has its own database that has no information in it. To run commands on it add `heroku run` to standard commands. For example, we should `migrate` our initial database and then create a superuser account.

Command Line

```
$ heroku run python manage.py migrate
$ heroku run python manage.py createsuperuser
```

There are two ways to open the newly-deployed application. From the command line you can type `heroku open -a` and the name of your app. Or you can click on the "Open app" button in the upper right corner of the Heroku dashboard.

Command Line

```
$ heroku open -a fast-ravine-89805
```

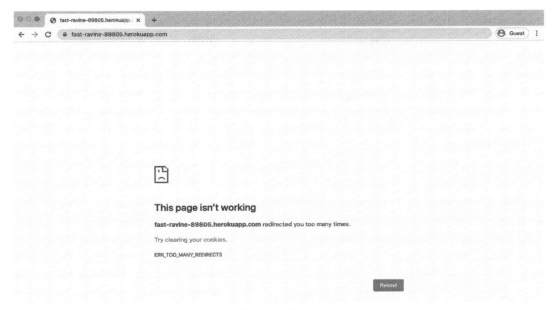

Heroku Redirects

But...ack! What's this? A redirect error. Welcome to the joys of deployment where issues like this will crop up all the time.

SECURE_PROXY_SSL_HEADER

Some sleuthing uncovers that the issue is related to our SECURE_SSL_REDIRECT[314] setting. Heroku uses proxies and so we must find the proper header and update SECURE_PROXY_-SSL_HEADER[315] accordingly.

By default it is set to `None`, but since we *do* trust Heroku we can update it (`'HTTP_X_FORWARDED_-PROTO'`, `'https'`). This setting won't harm us for local development so we'll add it directly into the `config/settings.py` file as follows:

---

[314] https://docs.djangoproject.com/en/3.1/ref/settings/#secure-ssl-redirect
[315] https://docs.djangoproject.com/en/3.1/ref/settings/#std:setting-SECURE_PROXY_SSL_HEADER

Code

```python
# config/settings.py
SECURE_PROXY_SSL_HEADER = ('HTTP_X_FORWARDED_PROTO', 'https') # new
```

Commit these change to Git and push the updated code to Heroku.

Command Line

```
$ git status
$ git commit -m 'secure_proxy_ssl_header and allowed_hosts update'
$ git push heroku master
```

After the build has completed refresh the webpage for your site. There it is!

Heroku Live Site

Heroku Logs

It is inevitable that you will have errors in your deployment at some point. When you do, run `heroku logs --tail` to see error and info logs and debug what's going on.

Hopefully this deployment process was smooth. But in practice, even with an established Platform-as-a-Service like Heroku, it is highly likely that issues will occur. If you see an error page, type `heroku logs --tail`, which displays info and error logs, to diagnose the issue.

Heroku Add-ons

Heroku comes with a large list of add-on services[316] that, for a fee, can be quickly added to any site. For example, to enable caching with Memcache, Memcachier[317] is an option to consider.

Daily backups[318] are an additional, but essential, feature of any production database.

And if you're using a custom domain for your site, ensuring SSL is vital for any website. You will need to be on a paid tier on Heroku[319] to enable this functionality.

Conclusion

There was a lot of code in this chapter so if you have any errors, please check the official source code on Github[320].

Even with all the advantages of a modern Platform-as-a-Service like Heroku, deployment remains a complicated and often frustrating task for many developers. Personally, I want my web apps to "just work". But many engineers come to enjoy the challenges of working on performance, security, and scaling. After all, it is far easier to measure improvements in this realm: did page load times decrease? Did site uptime improve? Is security up-to-date? Working on these problems can often feel far more rewarding than debating which new feature to add to the site itself.

---

[316] https://elements.heroku.com/addons/

[317] https://elements.heroku.com/addons/memcachier

[318] https://devcenter.heroku.com/articles/heroku-postgres-backups#scheduling-backups

[319] https://devcenter.heroku.com/articles/understanding-ssl-on-heroku

[320] https://github.com/wsvincent/djangoforprofessionals/tree/master/ch17-deployment

Conclusion

Building a "professional" website is no small task even with all the help that a batteries-included web framework like Django provides. Docker provides a major advantage in standardizing both local and production environments regardless of local machine–and especially in a team context. However Docker is a complicated beast on its own. While we have used it judiciously in this book there is much more that it can do depending on the needs of a project.

Django itself is friendly to small projects because its defaults emphasize rapid local development but these settings must be systematically updated for production, from upgrading the database to PostgreSQL, using a custom user model, environment variables, configuring user registration flow, static assets, email... on and on it goes.

The good news is that the steps needed for a production-level approach are quite similar. Hence the first half of this book is deliberately agnostic about the eventual project that is built: you'll find these steps are standard on almost any new Django project. The second half focused on building a real Bookstore site with modern best practices, added Reviews, image uploads, set permissions, added search, reviewed performance and security measures, and finally deployed on Heroku with containers.

For all the content covered in this book we've really only scratched the surface of what Django can do. This is the nature of modern web development: constant iteration.

Django is a magnificent partner in building out a professional website because so many of the considerations required have already been thought of and included. But knowledge is needed to know how to turn these production switches on to take full advantage of the customization Django allows. Ultimately that is the goal of this book: to expose you, the reader, to the full spectrum of what Django and professional websites require.

As you learn more about web development and Django I'd urge caution when it comes to premature optimization. It is always tempting to add features and optimizations to your project that you *think* you'll need later. The short list includes adding a CDN for static and media assets, judiciously analyzing database queries, adding indexes to models, and so on.

The truth is that in any given web project there will always be more to do than time allows. This book has covered the fundamentals that are worthy of upfront time to get right. Additional steps around security, performance, and features will present themselves to you in real-time. Try to resist the urge to add complexity until absolutely necessary.

Learning Resources

As you become more comfortable with Django and web development in general, you'll find the official Django documentation[321] and source code[322] increasingly valuable. I refer to both on an almost daily basis. There is also the official Django forum[323], a great resource albeit underutilized resource for Django-specific questions.

To continue on your Django journey, a good source of additional tutorials and courses is the website LearnDjango.com[324], which I maintain. There is also the weekly podcast, Django Chat[325], co-hosted by Django Fellow Carlton Gibson, and Django News[326], a weekly newsletter filled with the latest news, articles, and tutorials on Django.

Feedback

As a final note, I'd love to hear your thoughts about the book. It is a constant work-in-progress and the detailed feedback from readers helps me continue to improve it. I respond to every email and can be reached at will@learndjango.com[327].

If you purchased this book on Amazon, please consider leaving an honest review. These reviews make an enormous impact on book sales.

Thank you for reading the book and good luck on your journey with Django!

---

[321]https://www.djangoproject.com/
[322]https://github.com/django/django
[323]https://forum.djangoproject.com/
[324]https://learndjango.com
[325]https://djangochat.com
[326]https://django-news.com
[327]mailto:will@learndjango.com

Printed in Great Britain
by Amazon

64596716R00165